Negotiation Skills
for ROOKIES

Copyright © 2009 LID Editorial Empresarial and Marshall Cavendish Limited

First published in 2009 by

Marshall Cavendish Limited
Fifth Floor
32–38 Saffron Hill
London EC1N 8FH
United Kingdom
T: +44 (0)20 7421 8120
F: +44 (0)20 7421 8121
sales@marshallcavendish.co.uk
www.marshallcavendish.co.uk

A member of **BPR**

businesspublishersroundtable.com

Marshall Cavendish is a trademark of Times Publishing Limited

Other Marshall Cavendish offices: Marshall Cavendish International (Asia) Private Limited, 1 New Industrial Road, Singapore 536196 • Marshall Cavendish Corporation. 99 White Plains Road, Tarrytown NY 10591–9001, USA • Marshall Cavendish International (Thailand) Co Ltd. 253 Asoke, 12th Floor, Sukhumvit 21 Road, Klongtoey Nua, Wattana, Bangkok 10110, Thailand • Marshall Cavendish (Malaysia) Sdn Bhd, Times Subang, Lot 46, Subang Hi-Tech Industrial Park, Batu Tiga, 40000 Shah Alam, Selangor Darul Ehsan, Malaysia

A CIP record for this book is available from the British Library

ISBN 978-0-462-09953-8

Illustrations by Nuria Aparicio and Joan Guardiet

Printed and bound in Great Britain by
TJ International Limited, Padstow, Cornwall

Contents

Introduction

There can be no better place to start than with Annabel, aged 6, who is quoted in an internet newsletter as saying: "If you want a guinea pig, then you start by asking for a pony." This is indicative of wisdom way beyond the young lady's age, and – as we will see – of an apparently inherent understanding of a core principle of the process of negotiation. Doubtless Annabel has more to learn, but she is off to a good start.

Negotiation may seem, at first sight, like something that other people do. High-powered business people, politicians and union leaders negotiate. But, to put it more simply, they are *bargaining,* and all of us do that. When you bargain, and bargain successfully, you can smooth relations and save money, time, aggravation and face in many different situations.

The applications of bargaining, or negotiation, are wide; they include being used:

- As part of the sales process (by both buyer and seller).
- Between individuals for primarily personal reasons (for example, negotiating a pay increase or remuneration package, or "discussing" with your boss when you might go on holiday).
- In wage bargaining (such as between an employer organization and a union or staff group).

8
- In political circles (such as in treaties between governments).
- Internationally (either between individuals or organizations in different countries or literally on a worldwide basis – like the ongoing talks about measures to combat global warming).
- In corporate affairs (takeovers, mergers and a variety of alliances and collaborations, sought or forced by circumstances).

Negotiation often involves a financial element (though it may not) and it can involve two people or groups of people and take place at every level of an organizational hierarchy. Finally it may be momentary and minor – "If you can deputize for me at tomorrow's meeting, I can give you a little longer on that deadline we spoke about" – but still always needs getting right.

Negotiation is relevant to discussions between colleagues or people who do not know each other, people in the same organization or different ones, and people of different experience, background, nationality and outlook. The negotiating process involves balancing matters between two parties so that you not only get what you want (achieving this is down to persuasion), but get what you want in the best possible way. It is the art of concluding a deal, and the arrangement of all the elements that constitute that deal; the terms and conditions, for instance, in some business deals. It is a form of communication, and as such it is an interactive process. There is thus no single right approach, guaranteed to work no matter what, though there are certainly definite principles that can be used to form the basis of any success. What works for one situation may not be right for another, but what you find does work will probably help the next time you are in similar circumstances and must again find an appropriate way forward.

This short book sets out the essentials – what really matters – about the process. It reviews the core techniques and practical, proven approaches that provide a basis for undertaking negotiation, and

aims to make them understandable and manageable so that you can
quickly put your rookie status behind you. Given that this is a skill that
you can spend a lifetime developing, it also provides a basis from
which you can fine-tune in the future.

Above all, understanding and utilizing negotiation requires:

- A basis of sound, effective communications skills (because
  negotiation is a specialist form of communications).
- An understanding of the role of negotiation (because it is almost
  always part of a broader picture, for instance one that starts with
  persuasion).
- The ability to orchestrate a plethora of techniques and relate what
  is done to the particular meeting and circumstances (in other
  words, this is not something that can be applied by rote).
- A sensitivity to the people involved, as what is done must be based
  on an understanding of them and their situation.

A final, important point: remember that negotiation is a career skill
– that is, one affecting not only an individual's performance in their
job, but also probably influencing how they progress in their career. It
is a very personal skill and certainly one that can contribute to your
individual profile, and thus how people judge you in terms of capabili-
ties and professionalism.

First of all you need to read this book. But you not only need to
know something of the skills that are involved; you also need to practise them. This book is designed to help you make a start, at least with
the skills, and perhaps also to spur on your practice. I think it will help.
I want you to buy this book. You want to be a more effective negotiator.
This book will help you become just that – buy it and we both get what
we want. Is it a deal?

Negotiation is a complex process. That is not to say that it is intellectually taxing, but instead the complexity comes from the fact that there is a good deal to it; a good deal going on. So, the first thing that is necessary in addressing how to conduct negotiations is to have a clear overview of the process. Knowing what is involved makes it easier to tackle the deployment of individual elements of the process, each element of which is essentially a matter of common sense.

CHAPTER 1

Understanding the process

Negotiation in context

Why would you want to learn how to negotiate effectively? And what makes it such a complex skill? To answer these questions you need to understand exactly what negotiation is and how it works.

In so many discussions the conclusion cannot be a simple yes or no. There will always be many permutations and aspects to be discussed, which have to add up to an outcome acceptable to both, or all, parties. The process of achieving this may take some time. Each aspect has to be considered in turn; and, of course, different people have different ideas about what they want, what is reasonable and how to go about achieving agreement.

Negotiation is a very particular process, characterized in a number of ways.

- First, as we said before, it is complex. The complexity comes from the need to orchestrate a many-faceted process rather than because of anything intellectually taxing. But you need to be quick witted to keep all the necessary balls in the air, and you always need to see the broad picture while concentrating on individual details.

12 • Secondly, while negotiation is not to be treated as an argument (if it is, then an impasse usually results), nevertheless it *is* adversarial. Both parties involved want the best deal they can obtain. Yet compromise is essential: stick out for a perfect deal and the other party may walk away. Give way too easily and you may well regret what is then agreed. Both participants must be satisfied with what they do agree (the win–win option).

  • Thirdly, there is a ritual aspect to negotiation. It is a process that needs to be gone through. It takes time. There is to-and-fro debate, and a mutually agreeable solution needs to be seen to be being sought out, as well as actually taking place. Too much haste and a rush for agreement or a take-it-or-leave-it approach can fail – less because the deal it offers is unacceptable, more because the other party does not feel that the process is being taken seriously. People look for hidden meaning, believe that something better must be possible – and again the outcome can be stalemate.

Recognizing the adversarial aspect

There is certainly an adversarial aspect to negotiation. As the mid-twentieth century politician Lord Hore-Belisha famously once said: "When a man tells me he is going to put all his cards on the table, I always look up his sleeve." Both parties want to win. One of the tricks of successful negotiation, therefore, is for it to end with both sides feeling they have reached a satisfactory conclusion. The adversarial element must be kept in check so that discussions do not deteriorate into a slanging match, with both sides setting impossible conditions and no agreement likely. Negotiation is adversarial, but only by keeping that aspect under control can it lead to an acceptable outcome for you.

Rookie Buster

Negotiation is adversarial, but only by keeping that aspect under control can it lead to an acceptable outcome for you.

Partly because of this, negotiating involves a fair bit of give and take. You cannot proceed without having an understanding of the other party and their objectives. Ultimately you are after the best deal possible, rather than chasing something unrealistic. None of this happens without the process of to and fro discussion, and there is an element of ritual in this. There are conventions and ways of doing things, and unless you keep reasonably close to them, real progress may be jeopardized.

Where negotiating fits

By learning and deploying the techniques of negotiation you will save yourself or your organization time and money. Or you may simply put yourself in a stronger position to achieve what you want in discussion.

Several factors make for success; each is reviewed here in turn. A basic yet vital factor is that negotiation is a form of communication. Negotiation must work in communications terms before it can achieve its specific objectives – after all, you will not get people to agree to something they do not really understand. So make no mistake: if you do not communicate clearly you will never be a successful negotiator.

Rookie Buster

If you do not communicate clearly you will never be a successful negotiator.

14   In addition, persuasive communication and negotiation must work together in the right way. Several things are important here.

Communication (that is, making something clear) is never easy. Persuasive communication is harder still, and getting someone to do what you want can be downright difficult. Negotiation – agreeing the deal – is something else. The processes overlap. Communication is the continuing process, and within it persuasion normally comes first, as you have to get agreement first (there is no point in someone bothering about terms, conditions and other arrangements if they do not want a deal to start with). Negotiation follows agreement, although negotiation and persuasion can be in train together to some extent, especially in the early stages of a discussion. That said, before we get into the details about negotiation we must set the scene and deal with the basic skills from which it springs.

On an everyday basis, communication may seem easy. You do it all the time, with family, friends and day-to-day contacts of all kinds, as well as in a business context. Communication may be verbal or in writing. But communication may have inherent complications. For instance, consider the telephone; this poses problems because you cannot see people and judge their intentions or reactions from facial expressions. Such communication may be emotional, complex or hasty. Consider too the problems that sometimes occur with hastily composed emails. There is always a need for care and to avoid communications breakdown. Whatever form communication takes, it may run into problems because it is:

- Unclear.
- Imprecise and thus ambiguous.
- Incomplete or based on assumptions rather than facts.
- Full of jargon.

There are dozens of potential hazards; you may lose the thread of your argument, or the other person may not be listening. Classic examples of communication breakdown abound. A nice example of simple confusion is the classic sign in shops that says "Ears Pierced While You Wait" – there's some other way? And an American president, Richard Nixon, is credited with having said: "I know that you think you understand what you think I said, but I am not sure you realize that what you heard is not what I meant." You are certainly going to need to be clearer than that! This cannot be overstated. If you are clear and communicate with due precision you are more likely to carry others with you. It also contributes to you being seen as professional and a force to be reckoned with – clear communication is the first foundation for successful negotiation.

Rookie Buster

Clear communication is the first foundation for successful negotiation.

If people are not clear about what you mean, you cannot hope to move on to the next stage, that of persuading them, which is the precursor to negotiating.

Being persuasive

Providing a communication is made clear, then it can then be made persuasive. Being persuasive, in turn, depends on the right approach. And this must be based on the point of view, and thinking, of the other person. It is very easy for communication to end up unpersuasive because it is no more than your saying "do this". With no consideration of the other person or their point of view you are unlikely to make persuasion work. You want action, but this will only follow if the other person understands, and appreciates and sees the need for it. So understanding other people underpins success in being persuasive: you do best if you view being persuasive as "helping people to make a decision" rather than as something you do "to" them.

Rookie Buster

Understanding other people underpins success in being persuasive: you do best if you view being persuasive as "helping people to make a decision" rather than as something you do "to" them.

While you need to state your case and regard what happens as *your* communication, you will only get your way if people on the receiving end find it acceptable. If they believe you are trying to do something "to" them, to persuade them against their will, agreement will be difficult. On the other hand, if they feel you have their interests in mind, things will proceed better. Let's start by looking at the thinking process involved when considering someone's request for action. Based on psychological studies in the USA, this process is often described as one that moves through seven stages:

1. I am important and I want to be respected.
2. Consider my needs.
3. How will your ideas/proposition help me?
4. What are the facts?
5. What are the snags?
6. What shall I do?
7. I approve (or not).

This seems like common sense. Indeed, it is what you do in all manner of situations in which a decision needs to be made. You weigh up the case or argument, put all the good points on one side, all the less good on the other and assess the net effect. The image of a balance or weighing scales on which the plus and minus points – large and small – are placed progressively as a case is considered is a good one to keep in mind.

Any attempt at communication that results in an unsatisfactory response to any of the seven stages outlined above is unlikely to end in agreement. The mind must be satisfied on each point before considering the next. To be successful the persuasive process must match, and run parallel with, the decision-making sequence. The chart below shows how both sides relate and what their objectives are at each stage.

Decision sequence	Persuasion objectives	Persuasion stages
I am important/Consider my needs	To create rapport, generate interest or acceptance, and find out about them	Opening
What are the facts?	To state a case that will be seen as balanced in favour of action	Stating the case
What are the snags?	Preventing or handling negative reactions that may unbalance the argument	Handling objections
What shall I do?/ I approve	Obtaining a commitment to action, or to a step in the right direction	Injunction to act

Among the many techniques of persuasion, matching the other person's decision-making thoughts, and describing your own case in a way that reflects them, is key in influencing results. Persuasion may fail if the detail here is not respected. The sequence and the totality of the process must be accommodated, and the pace at which the decider is going must be broadly matched. Going too fast can be self-defeating and result in a don't-push-me response. The aim is always a commitment to act, or to achieve a firm step on the way to that ultimate goal.

Rookie Buster

Going too fast can be self-defeating and result in a don't-push-me response.

18   Consider an example of how a variety of stages can be involved: a secretary wants her boss to buy her a new and better computer. Her ultimate objective is for him to say "Yes, buy it" about a particular machine. A useful step may be to persuade him to review some brochures, arrange and attend a demonstration or obtain a firm quotation. All such steps can be the basis of specific objectives: she may decide that the first thing to do is to get him to agree to a demonstration. Sometimes there are many such steps to be gone through before the ultimate objective is reached. Getting agreement to each of these becomes a worthwhile goal in itself.

Managing the process

Whatever the ultimate objective, part of what ensures that persuasion works is thinking ahead; anticipating how the decision will be made, and what factors are most important. Questioning techniques will be important to this process; more on this later.

A successful outcome does not always emerge from one contact between those involved. Several meetings or exchanges may be necessary. When there is a multiplicity of contacts, each stage has its own sequence to be followed, as does the whole process.

You always need to plan ahead if communication is to run smoothly and objectives are to be achieved. Although you cannot predict exactly what the responses will be, anticipating them as accurately as possible will always help. This does not imply adopting a scripted or parrot-like approach: rather it means that you intend to direct the conversation towards a specific conclusion.

Rookie Buster

You always need to plan ahead if communication is to run smoothly.

It may help to think of this graphically. Imagine the helmsman of a yacht, sailing across an open sea and subject to the impact of wind and tide. He might take a number of courses, though imagining a straight line to the chosen destination will allow him to correct course and keep on track.

Another issue must be touched on. It should already be clear that, if persuasion is to succeed, you need to keep a clear eye on the listener and their point of view. Your whole approach must come over as acceptable and not seem over-assertive or even aggressive and thus risk switching people off. So, the next issue is making things acceptable.

Projecting an acceptable manner

The way communications generally, and especially persuasion and negotiating, are received is influenced to a considerable extent by the persona and style of the person doing the communicating. Think about how quickly you switch off from someone to whom you take a dislike for some reason. How you come over is as important as what you do; if you appear to be professional, then people will judge you accordingly and take you more seriously – which means that you need to actively cultivate the right persona.

Rookie Buster

If you appear to be professional, then people will judge you accordingly and take you more seriously.

20   Two factors combine to make your manner acceptable. These are:
1. Projection.
2. Empathy.

Projection means the way you come over to others – particularly the confidence, credibility and influence you convey. **Empathy** simply means the ability to put yourself in another person's shoes and to see things from their point of view: and not merely to see them, but to let the other person understand that you are doing so.

Recognizing different types of communicator

You can consider four distinct types of communicator on an axis of high and low projection, and high and low empathy. They are:

Type 1 – Low in empathy, but high in projection
This high-pressure communicator is over-aggressive and insensitive. They may feel they win the argument, but their projection without empathy becomes self-defeating and switches people off. For many people, an archetypal high-pressure communicator might be, say, a secondhand car salesman.

Type 2 – Low in empathy and projection
This take-it-or-leave-it communicator has little interest in either the other person or even their own ideas. A lack of commitment to the whole process tends to let it run into the sand. The archetypal take-it-or-leave-it communicator, someone most of us are familiar with, is the unhelpful shop assistant.

Type 3 – High in empathy, but low in projection
This weak communicator is the sort of whom it is said disparagingly that they mean well. And so they do. They have good sensitivity to other people; they come over as essentially nice. However, they tend to

take the side of the listener so much that persuasion vanishes and they achieve no commitment.

Type 4 – High in both

This ideal communicator has a creative understanding of the listener. He is well informed and produces both agreement and commitment to the satisfaction of both sides. Being seen to see the other person's point of view is crucial.

Achieving the correct blend of empathy and projection is important. Both elements are necessary, but either can be under or overdone. If you get the balance right, the other person will find your approach reasonable and acceptable. This is not only important for communication and persuasion, but it is also the approach that you will need if you are to negotiate successfully.

Clearly there is more to being persuasive than just getting the balance of empathy and projection right. Exactly how one goes through the seven stages of consideration, and the techniques involved, is also important. Persuasive communication is the second foundation for successful negotiation.

Rookie Buster

Persuasive communication is the second foundation for successful negotiation.

Towards negotiation

Only when someone has been persuaded in principle towards a particular course of action will they be interested in moving on to make any sort of deal. If you have communicated clearly and achieved understanding, and if you have succeeded in being truly persuasive and there is essentially agreement to proceed, then you can move on to the process of negotiation itself.

22 In real life, the processes of persuasion and negotiation overlap. There is no sharp division between them. Often a complete cycle of interaction takes place, as was described earlier, with communication going on throughout. Whilst the approach described, operating from the basis of a sound appreciation of the other person's point of view, is the beginning of being effective in this area, there is much more to it than that. The process of communication needs working at, and communicating persuasively needs working at even more. It must be made manageable. It needs planning and structuring. And you must always be acutely conscious of what is going on, because you never know how people will react.

Rookie Buster

You must always be acutely conscious of what is going on, because you never know how people will react.

An example will help to make this clear.

Judging the situation

Let's consider the sales operation of an organization. It is a charity which is focused on raising money for its cause and keeping internal costs down. Staffing is therefore tight. Recent changes have included moving their major revenue earner, the catalogue operation, selling everything from greetings cards to gifts, from an external site into the main building.

Martin makes a complaint 23

Martin runs the catalogue order office. One of his main preoccupations is customer service, and he finds that the switchboard is not servicing his department efficiently. Despite having a note of who handles what, the switchboard is misrouting many calls, resulting in constant transfers and customers being upset. This is especially important in a charity, as any inefficiency is quickly associated with waste of money.

Martin writes a memo to the administration manager complaining that the lack of efficiency is upsetting customers, risking the loss of orders and revenue, and damaging the organization's good image.

Rose is defensive

Rose is the administration manager. She is busy, especially so with the changes and the seemingly endless need to keep staffing tight. She has 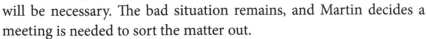 only met Martin once, when his department moved in, and has little knowledge of his part of the overall operation.

Rose knows the switchboard operators are hard pressed. She defends them strongly, suggesting Martin takes steps to better inform customers about who they should ask for. She returns to what she sees as more pressing matters, hoping no more action will be necessary. The bad situation remains, and Martin decides a meeting is needed to sort the matter out.

Achieving a resolution

As Martin plans the meeting, his objective is clear: service must be improved. He quickly realizes, however, that it is not a matter of issuing instructions, or even of persuasion. He has to work with Rose, and accepts that establishing smooth relations between them is also an

24   objective. He realizes that attitudes have caused the problem to esca-
late because:

- He saw the situation as a simple instruction: "Make the change."
- She saw only the criticism and became defensive, leaving the ball
  in Martin's court.

Martin realizes he must negotiate. First-class standards of service
are vital. But the switchboard operators probably do have a problem.
After all, the new catalogue department has perhaps doubled the
number of calls they answer. There needs to be some give and take. He
begins to list what he could do:

- Prepare an easy check reference to go in front of each operator,
  showing who does what.
- Brief the switchboard operators personally on the action
  necessary.
- Explain the importance of these new calls. After all, they give the
  operators a chance to influence fund raising very directly: good
  service means more orders.
- Check the order forms to see whether amendments could make
  things clearer in future.
- Offer to keep the two groups of staff in touch. Perhaps the
  switchboard operators could each have a tour of the order office
  to show them what goes on there, and how they are really part of
  the same team.

In return Martin needs to ask for some priority for customer calls,
at the expense of certain other tasks. It is not yet clear what this might
involve, but it might mean some reorganization. There is a balance to
be struck, which is why Martin needs to think about what concessions
he may offer. Perhaps the first job is to persuade Rose that it is potentially something that can help them both. Despite the immediate
aggravations the situation poses, in the long term there could be more
job interest and motivation for her. Both parties will come out of the
ensuing exchange better if they avoid reacting precipitately or emo-
tionally and see the situation for what it is: negotiation. If they approach
their discussions in this way, then a solution is likely to be satisfactory

to everyone. Situations can be mishandled as much by failure to nego- 25
tiate as by negotiating badly.

Rookie Buster

Situations can be mishandled as much by failure to
negotiate as by negotiating badly.

Coach's notes

To make negotiation work for you, you must:
- Understand how negotiation relates to communication generally, and to persuasive communication in particular, so that you can make everything play its part.
- Recognize that communicating clearly is an important component of negotiation; in fact no negotiation is possible if one party does not understand exactly what the other is saying.

Already you may be able to link what you have read in this chapter to your own situation. Having an example (the kind of thing you must do) in mind as you read on will help you link theory and practice.

Go for it! Why do people who excel at something make you marvel at their apparently effortless expertise? It is unlikely to be because they are "naturals" and born to it – more probably it is simply because they work at it. That means practice and, crucially, making sure you understand the fundamentals. There is too much going on when something like negotiation is in progress to have your attention distracted trying to figure out the basics.

So don't neglect this level of understanding – making sure you have a clear, thorough grasp of the underlying principles is the first step to developing your skills.

28

Notes

Notes

Negotiation is undoubtedly complex, but here you will get to the core of what makes it work, particularly the concepts of win–win negotiation and of trading variables. Next we will review the question of preparation, and then the various tactics and strategies that will give your negotiating technique the edge are laid out.

CHAPTER 2

Deploying the core techniques

Defining the process

There is more to negotiating than at first meets the eye. First of all, consider what negotiation is not. For a start, it is not simply stating a grievance. Imagine that your toaster has come back from the menders but it is still doing its best to cremate your toast. Most people would complain instinctively, but often without proposing any remedy. At best, complaints produce apologies. At worst, they produce arguments in which threats produce counter-threats, and this can ultimately result in an impasse. All too often communication can end up this way. It starts with complaints ("Productivity in your department is drop-ping," "Sales results are below target") and then deteriorates into an argument – "No, it's not," "There are good reasons for that," and so on. What you really want in such circumstances is action. You have to suggest, or prompt, a proposal: something that will put things right. Arguments cannot be negotiated, only proposals can. This, in turn, demands that emotions are kept under control. Always remember that negotiation is a delicate business, one which you need to think about carefully, both before and during the process.

Rookie Buster

Negotiation is a delicate business, one which you need to think about carefully, both before and during the process.

Win–win negotiation

It is inherent to the process of negotiation that *both* the parties involved end up feeling satisfied that they have struck an appropriate deal. It may not be exactly the result they both hoped for, but it is one they can realistically agree to. It is this outcome that gives rise to the description of what is called a "win–win" negotiating situation. Win–win negotiation recognizes the realities of the process and accepts that matters must end with some degree of satisfaction for both parties.

Rookie Buster

Win–win negotiation recognizes the realities of the process and accepts that matters must end with some degree of satisfaction for both parties.

Some individuals feel they must win every point, deliberately creating a win–lose approach. Negotiation is, however, a process of some give and take, and if both parties accept this, then a win–win approach is more likely to achieve a productive conclusion. Consider the implications. For instance, in win–win negotiation:

- Seek out common ground, rather than insisting that everything goes your way.

- Relate to the other party and their concerns, rather than just objecting to them.
- Be ready to compromise, at least to some degree, rather than remaining inflexible.
- Allow discussion to accommodate to-and-fro debate, rather than insisting on a rigid agenda.
- Ensure discussion includes questioning – and thus listening – rather than just stating your case.
- Disclose appropriate information, rather than maintaining total secretiveness.
- Build relationships, not bad feelings.
- Aim for agreement and not stalemate.

A win–win conclusion should normally be your aim. Complexities demand care. You have to keep a number of elements in mind if the process is to move along satisfactorily. Overall, negotiation is the process of identifying, arranging and agreeing the terms and conditions, whatever they may be, of a deal.

Rookie Buster

Negotiation is the process of identifying, arranging and agreeing the terms and conditions, whatever they may be, of a deal.

Remember that persuasive communication starts the process. This is where one party puts across their case and, in their own mind, the other person begins to accept it, even if nothing is openly agreed at this stage. As agreement in principle begins to emerge, the question switches from "Will this person agree?" to "On what basis will they agree?" Each party is then concerned that every detail making up the deal will suit them as much as possible. It will probably be impossible for both to be 100 per cent satisfied, but the balance must be right.

34 *Trading and using variables*

"Variables" are the raw material of negotiation. They may indeed be many and various, and this contributes to the overall complexity of the negotiation process.

An everyday example will illustrate the point. Imagine you are going to make some major household purchase: a refrigerator, perhaps. Which model you buy, and from where, will depend on a number of factors, and perhaps a surprisingly large number of them – these are the variables. Price is one, of course. But there are many other factors about the fridge itself: the star rating of its freezer unit; the size, number and arrangement of shelves; the bottle-holding capacity; the colour; which way the door opens; and so on. There may also be other, less obvious factors. How much does it cost to run? Will the supplier deliver it, and by when – and with what certainty? Will they carry it up to a third floor apartment? What payment terms are available? What guarantee and service arrangements apply? You can no doubt think of more. This kind of purchase may consist only of checking and considering such factors and then making a decision, but some of the factors may not be fixed. Some will be offered – or not – by the shop from the outset, while others have to be suggested and negotiated. Some things will only be included in the deal after they have been suggested, discussed and agreed.

Once this process is involved, balance becomes necessary. Both parties may need to give as well as take. You may agree to delay delivery by two weeks, for example, and in return they will deliver free of charge, when they have a van coming your way. They may agree to take a percentage off the price if you pay cash. And so on. In other words, you "trade variables". You swap them to balance and re-balance the deal. Such trading may use all or part of a variable: for instance, you might agree to collect the fridge, forgoing any kind of delivery, but receiving a bigger discount on the price. Of course some options and decisions preclude negotiating: buy from a website, for instance, and the price may be right, but the deal is fixed. This gives us another principle to keep in mind: understanding, identifying, assessing and trading variables are at the core of negotiation and above all what can get you a good deal. We will look at the techniques of trading variables in more detail later.

Rookie Buster

Understanding, identifying, assessing and trading variables are at the core of negotiation and above all what can get you a good deal.

Assessing the raw materials of negotiation

Variables are the raw materials of negotiation. Each one has a scale of possible decisions on which you must settle and agree. For example:

- Discount: none, or 10, 15, 25, 50 per cent…?
- Delivery: this afternoon, at exactly 3pm, this week, next week…?

There are often many variables; you need a clear idea of the relative importance of different ones and of what position on the scale is likely to be acceptable to both sides. The more variables there are, and the harder they are to prioritize, the more complex the negotiation becomes. The human interactions inherent in the process complicate the negotiation.

36 # *Increasing the likelihood of success*

If you are not careful, you may look back after a meeting and conclude that you lost out. Perhaps you failed to recognize the need for negotiation. In that case, you will have handled the transaction inadequately and the end result is likely to have been a bad deal. For example, an administration manager may telephone a supplier to complain about an incorrectly completed service on a company car. The complaint may produce no more than an apology. If the manager really wants something done about it, he or she must suggest a remedy: maybe balancing the inconvenience of the car going back to the service centre against the seriousness of any fault and the option of leaving it until the next service. Many different approaches are possible here, and different arrangements may result from all of them. If you see something as negotiation, but go at it like a bull at a gate, or focus exclusively on a single element or allow the transaction to develop into an argument, you are unlikely to achieve what you want.

Rookie Buster

If you focus exclusively on a single element or allow the transaction to develop into an argument, you are unlikely to achieve what you want.

Success in negotiation rests primarily on three interrelated fundamentals:

- What you do. The techniques and processes that are involved.
- How you go about it. The manner you employ and the effects this has on those with whom you negotiate.
- Preparation. The first two fundamentals are both dependent on preparation. Preparing for negotiation is a matter of common sense. Yet it is easier said than done. Probably more negotiators fail to reach the best arrangement for want of adequate

preparation than for any other reason. This links to two further important points.

At this stage it is useful to keep in mind an old saying, to remind you that a positive approach is essential. Remember: you don't get what you deserve, you get what you negotiate.

Rookie Buster

You don't get what you deserve, you get what you negotiate.

Success does have to be earned. It was Vidal Sassoon who said "The only place where success comes before work is in the dictionary." Success in negotiation, as in so much else in life, does not just happen by itself. People with good skills in this area tend to make it look easy. A good cook or a skilful public speaker makes what they do seem effortless, but a good deal of preparation will have gone into creating this impression. Accepting that some preparation is always necessary, however long or short the process may need to be, is the first step to success.

Creating an edge

Furthermore (and this may help to persuade you if preparation sounds like a bit of a chore), sound preparation can give you your first edge in negotiation. In fact, preparation will, almost regardless of other factors, give you a head start in comparison with someone else who has not prepared thoroughly.

Rookie Buster

Preparation will, almost regardless of other factors, give you a head start in comparison with someone else who has not prepared thoroughly.

So it pays to do your homework, because such an edge is often vital. In many kinds of negotiation no quarter is given! Think how vigorous some international negotiations are, or some wage-bargaining discussions. A great deal may hang on the outcome, and the negotiator needs to have every trick of the trade on their side in order to stay on top.

Coach's notes

By now, you should be ready to pitch into negotiation and make it work for you. There is still plenty more to learn, but at this stage you already:

- Know the importance of preparation (there's more about this in Chapter 3).
- Understand that by aiming for a win–win outcome, you are more likely to get a deal you find satisfactory.
- Recognize that variables and the trading of variables is central to the tactics you will need to use.

However complicated it may all still seem, things should at least be starting to fall into place.

Go for it! In any negotiation you need to gain as much of an edge as possible. For example, it is any buyer's job to get the best possible deal for their organization. That is what they are paid for; the buyers are not on the sales people's side, and they will attempt to get the better of them in any way they can, especially on price.

Buyers really are there, at least in part, to apply pressure to get the best deal. And not just buyers – anyone you find yourself negotiating with could be like this. They will be intent on fighting their corner and meeting their objectives, financial or otherwise, and they will do their best for their position – not yours. Never underestimate the skill or resolve of those with whom you negotiate; if you assume anything, assume that you need to pull out all the stops.

Preparing, and preparing sufficiently thoroughly to influence what you do, is well worth the effort.

Notes

Preparation: the very word may make you twitch. It's a chore. You wonder if it is necessary. Why bother? You are sure you can wing it. But just pause and consider: this chapter will show you why it is necessary, how to go about it – and, above all, what a positive advantage it can give you.

CHAPTER 3

The nearest thing to a magic formula: preparation

Why prepare?

Do you think of yourself as inexperienced at – and perhaps even wary of – the process of negotiation? If so, this is probably, at least in part, because you are ill prepared. Being well prepared breeds confidence, and that alone will change your thinking. And confidence allows you to take control of the process in a way that an ad hoc approach will never do. Moreover, confidence will be read by others as competence; the way you appear is very important, as you will discover later.

If preparation is important, then the next question concerns how to go about preparing to negotiate. Preparation may constitute just a few moments' thought prior to the start of a conversation. Or it may be a few minutes or an hour or two of homework. Or it may mean sitting at a table with colleagues, thrashing out the best way forward and sometimes even rehearsing what will be done. Whatever scale of preparation circumstances dictate, the nature of the negotiation process means it must always take place – from the outset preparation can quite literally give you what others may feel is an "unfair" advantage. And wouldn't you rather have the advantage, whether fair or "unfair", on your side?

44

Rookie Buster

Preparation can quite literally give you what others may feel is an "unfair" advantage.

Relating to others

Preparation cannot be done in a vacuum. You need to consider:
- The other people involved.
- Your own position.

The first stage of preparation is to consider the person (or people) with whom you must negotiate and, if appropriate, the organization they represent. Negotiation may take place with all sorts of people: customers, suppliers, business colleagues (or your boss, or subordinates) and with people you may or may not know personally. Questions need to be answered about such people, for example:
- What role and/or intentions do they have?
- What needs (subjective and objective) do they have?
- What problems will they raise? What objections will they make?
- Can they decide things, or must they consult with someone else?

Each situation will raise different issues, but the principle of thinking through how people may handle something is similar in each case. Do not overlook this, or assume familiarity makes it unnecessary. Even with people you know and deal with regularly, such analysis may pay dividends.

As an example, consider negotiating with a banquet manager. Suppose you are making arrangements with the banquet manager at a hotel or conference centre to accommodate the annual general meeting of your organization. You want the meeting to go well. You want the arrangements to be appropriate. You want it to be memorable. The banquet manager wants it to go well too, of course, but they are also concerned that it should fit in with other functions, be easy to staff and

be profitable. For your part, you must be sure the banquet manager has 45
sufficient authority to make the arrangements you want, that they are
professional and knowledgeable, and that what they say is possible will
prove to be so on the day. Suppose the manager suggests a combina-
tion of rooms A and B. You feel B and C would suit better. Is their
suggestion based on how your group will be best accommodated, or to
allow the fitting in of the local football club in room C? And do you
want the football club next door anyway? As each element such as cost
and catering is discussed and various options reviewed, your growing
knowledge of the banquet manager and their intentions will allow you
to negotiate more successfully with them than if you knew nothing
about them. The two of you may never have met before, but some
consideration of what they are likely to be feeling and planning will
always help. This is true of whoever you deal with. Remember the old
saying: know thy enemy.

Rookie Buster

Remember the old saying: know thy enemy.

The other party is you, of course. How you are seen is important,
too. People will respect you more if they feel you appear professional
or expert, if you clearly have the authority to negotiate, if you appear
prepared, confident and in charge. You may never be quite as close to
this ideal as you would like, but often the other person has no way of
knowing this, and "appear" is the crucial word. Some people seem to
have the confidence to tell you black is white and make you believe it.
The one area in which appearances are not enough is preparation. You
must really be prepared – though of course it does no harm to appear
even better prepared than you actually are. All of this means that it is
essential to think matters through thoroughly.

46

Rookie Buster

You must really be prepared – though of course it does no harm to appear even better prepared than you actually are.

Setting objectives

If you have your objectives firmly in mind – and this is key – surely there is no problem in making them clear? But if you simply say "I want the best deal possible," then this provides nothing tangible to work with. There is all the difference in the world between an author saying, "Let's see if the editor will pay me more for my next article," and that author actually setting out to obtain a 10 per cent increase in the fee.

Remember the example of the annual general meeting. Making objectives clear is an important starting point. Briefly, the objectives for the annual general meeting were that it should be:

- Successful (and this could be defined in more detail).
- Felt by everyone to be appropriate in style and purpose.
- Memorable and impressive: setting the standard for years to come.

But there is more. What about cost? Are these objectives to be met regardless of cost, or do they have to be achieved within a budget? And what about audio-visual equipment and visual aids? This introduces another area of variables, and another scale against which matters must be judged and settled. The answer might be that the objectives are not regardless of cost, but that the budget must be realistic if what is wanted is to be achieved satisfactorily. Similarly, if visual aids are vital, the date of the meeting itself could be changed to secure a larger and better equipped meeting room, where the right equipment can easily be accommodated and a more professional show can be put on.

Setting realistic objectives

In negotiation you need to identify and set specific (and thus measurable) objectives. You need to have your priorities clear, and also clearly related to what variables are involved, and to understand your attitude to each. For example, are there some variables about which you are prepared to compromise, and if so, how far? And are there others about which you intend to be immovable?

You may want to consider another key factor – timing.

- Are you intent on achieving everything at once, in one meeting?
- Or is there a long-term strategy involved?

Systematic objective setting

Whatever you plan to negotiate about, and however it is to be done, the purpose must be clear. You must be able to answer the question "Why am I doing this?" and set out a purpose – one that involves both you and whoever you are to negotiate with, and that describes what effect you aim to have on them and what the outcome should ideally be.

Rookie Buster

Whatever you plan to negotiate about, and however it is to be done, the purpose must be clear.

48   Objectives need to be not only clear, but also spelled out in sufficient detail (certainly in your own mind and sometimes also for others who may be involved with you). They must act as a genuine guide to what you will do. They also need to not just reflect what you want, but also to recognize the two-sided nature of the negotiation process.

At this point we need to be SMART. This stands for:

- Specific.
- Measurable.
- Achievable.
- Realistic.
- Timed.

For example, if you are planning a presentation, you might regard your objectives as:

- *Specific*. Ensuring that your presentation comes over in a way that audiences will see as appropriate and informative.
- *Measurable*. Ensuring that action takes place afterwards. (You might set any appropriate measure for this: from agreements or actions that group members take or commit to, to the volume of applause you receive!)
- *Achievable*. Right for the audience: sufficient, understandable information in manageable form that really allows people to change and improve what they do.
- *Realistic*. Keeping the work involved proportionate to the benefit – for example, a short text (if it took you several days to read, the effort might prove greater than any benefit from it).
- *Timing*. Setting deadlines – always a good factor to include in any objective. By when are you going to finish reading this chapter? When is your next presentation? How far ahead of it should you prepare?

So ask yourself whether you are clear about your objectives even before you begin to prepare. If you know why the negotiation is to happen, and what you intend to achieve, then you are well on the way to success.

Rookie Buster

If you know why the negotiation is to happen, and what you intend to achieve, then you are well on the way to success.

Time spent making sure you have a clear vision of your objectives is time well spent. It may only take a few moments, or it may need more thought and take more time. Either way, it is still worth doing and in any case may well save time at later stages of preparation.

The reason for thinking through your objectives is not academic. If you are clear and confident about them, you will be able to conduct the kind of meeting that will allow you to reach them. Remember: "ready, aim, fire" is always likely to be the best order in which to proceed!

Rookie Buster

"Ready, aim, fire" is always likely to be the best order in which to proceed!

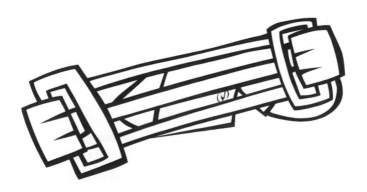

50 *Planning the structure of the meeting*

The preparation we have talked about so far is designed to influence the way in which a meeting will work. In fact, your preparation should anticipate all the factors that make up the complexities of negotiation. Preparation also includes matters relevant to the topic that the negotiation is to do with. For example, you may need to think how to justify your arguments as you explain your point of view. This goes back to general communication and any particular focus it may have; for example, the need to be persuasive. As you have seen, the variable factors of negotiation are, in effect, traded. (You may find the jargon here confusing, as people often use "variable" and "concession" to mean the same thing; that is, simply something that can be changed and agreed in different ways during a negotiation. The confusion comes because the word "concession" is also used when the variable is agreed on a particular basis where one party gives, or appears to give, some advantage to the other as this is done, thus making a concession.) But here the important point is that you will handle this give-and-take process much better if you have thought through some of the options – and there may be many of them.

Let's go back to the example of the booking a room for an AGM at a conference centre. The organizer might say to the banquet manager, "If we start an hour later, and choose an alternative menu, can we have the larger room at the same cost?" Here three elements – timing, menu and room options – are being used together in relation to overall cost, all contained within one short sentence.

The discussion could get very much more complicated than that, hence the need to have a firm, logical structure to keep everything under control during a meeting. By "structure", I mean the shape and to some extent the style of the meeting. Structure encompasses everything that will avoid any sort of muddle.

- What do you envisage happening?
- What will you aim to do first, second and third?

Having a clear and logical structure in mind helps you keep control

of the meeting and of all the disparate elements that you bring to the   51
table.

Rookie Buster

Having a clear and logical structure in mind helps you keep control of the meeting.

You need to consider the likely, or planned, duration of the meeting. For example, do you have one hour for discussion, or several hours, or must everything be agreed more promptly? Your order of sequence and priority must fit within the duration of the meeting. You will need to be very clear which are primary and which are secondary matters. If time runs short you do not want to find you have omitted anything of primary concern. A well-written report has a beginning, a middle and end; so does a good presentation. Both may require a detailed structure within each main segment, however, and a negotiation meeting is just the same.

Anticipating the tone of the meeting

As well as what you want to do, you need to think of how you want the meeting to go in terms of manner and feeling. For example, there may be stages at which you wish to be seen as particularly reasonable (or the opposite), and stages when you need to come over with some real heavyweight clout. What kind of personal profile do you wish to project? Make sure that your negotiating style is not in conflict with this. One should enhance the other.

While preparation is important, do not set what you intend to do in stone. You must retain a degree of flexibility throughout. You can never know for sure what the other party will do, but a clear plan still helps. It sets out your intention: what you would like to do. But think of your plan as a route map, not a straitjacket. Good planning should not prevent you being flexible and responding to circumstances. Indeed it should make it easier to do so. On a road journey, a map does not prevent you from changing your route if you unexpectedly find road works in the way. On the contrary, it helps you both divert and get back on track. At the risk of repetition, let's be clear – preparation is the foundation of successful negotiation.

Rookie Buster

Preparation is the foundation of successful negotiation.

Negotiation does not just happen, nor does the detail of how the meeting needs to progress. As you review the conduct of negotiation, both the shape of the meeting and the detail within that shape will become clearer. Remember:

- Negotiation involves more than one party; a win–win approach tends to do best for both.
- Variables are the raw material of negotiating, and success rests to a large extent on how you handle them. If you do not know where you are going, it is difficult to proceed with precision, so setting clear objectives is a prerequisite for success.

All this means that you should prepare carefully, both what you will do and how you will do it, and take a view of both sides of the situation.

Rookie Buster

If you do not know where you are going, it is difficult to proceed with precision.

Coach's notes

Preparation must not be skimped, and assessing the variables is an important part of it. You need to ask yourself:

- What variables do your own negotiation meetings involve? For any meeting you contemplate, these must be worked out in advance.
- Are you overlooking any possibilities?
- How much preparation should you do?
- What form should this preparation take?
- Would a colleague acting as a sounding board be useful?

Take time to think all this through, and make notes. You may want to keep your notes hidden from the person with whom you are negotiating, but if it will be useful to check the point you are going to make, then have the necessary details to hand during the meeting. One example of this is with calculations: it can be impressive if, anticipating something as you plan, you can glance (unobtrusively) at your notes and say something like, "I don't think 13.5 per cent does the trick – that's only £15,300!"

Go for it! Never underestimate the time you need to prepare, or how useful doing this can be. It was said in the Second World War that "Time spent in reconnaissance is seldom wasted." In wartime it helped you not to get killed, in negotiating it gives you what a less well prepared opponent might regard as an unfair advantage. Doing your homework is literally the first step to clinching a good deal.

Notes

Here the core of the negotiating process – trading variables or concessions – is reviewed, showing how to identify them and prioritize them,
and the precise way in which to go about trading to get the best from
what you do. This core process contributes significantly to the quality
of the ultimate deal you make.

CHAPTER 4

Using and trading variables

Categorizing variables

Negotiating variables may be at the core of the negotiating process, but not all variables are identical: they differ both in nature and potential. Similarly, their roles in trading may vary. Linking them to your plan and objectives will show you their potential role in the subsequent proceedings. Three types of variable are usually highlighted. They are:

- *The must-haves:* Those factors you feel you must bring away from the negotiation if the deal is to be at all acceptable to you.
- *The ideals:* Those factors which you would like to achieve, and which would constitute the ideal agreement. Realistically, these must include factors around which you are prepared to make some compromise.
- *The loss leaders:* Loss leaders take their name from products sold in stores at nil or negative profit margins simply to draw in buyers; the buyers then create profit by purchasing additional products on their visit. In negotiation "loss leaders" mean those aspects you are prepared to trade with, even if you would ideally

58 prefer not to, in order to clinch a deal. You need to regard some things as being in this category.

The ritual trading process must be involved; without it stalemate may easily result.

Rookie Buster

The ritual trading process must be involved; without it stalemate may easily result.

Trading is fundamental to negotiation. There is, in a way, a ritual to be completed, and without that no progress is possible. If all you do is state an unchangeable position and refuse to move, the outcome may be permanent stalemate. Some say this was what caused Edward Heath's downfall as Prime Minister years ago. During a major miners' strike he did just this. Believing his first offer (from which he refused to deviate) could not, by definition, be his last, the miners dug in their heels. There was effectively no negotiation, and ultimately the government toppled (maybe Heath should have studied negotiation and simply needed a Rookies guide!). Keeping what you have to work with in mind, you can now turn to the tactical principles that will help you conduct an effective meeting.

Starting to trade early on

Trading concessions may well – and often should – start early on in a negotiating meeting. Even if the trading initially reflects peripheral issues, it can still set the scene for what follows. Avoid giving anything – certainly anything significant – away too early. Even saying, "Why don't we talk this through over lunch? My treat," may give the wrong impression. Better to say, "If you agree to come to an agreement today,

then I will buy us lunch and we can chat this through in comfort." If
this kind of swap is handled informally, then no one need feel boxed
in. The conversation can move naturally to a more businesslike level.
Then the trading can really start. Use trading variables to get the negotiating process under way and on track.

Rookie Buster

Use trading variables to get the negotiating process
under way and on track.

Trading concessions: the rules

Trading can take the form of tentative exploration, as in the example
above, or be on what is called an "if A, then B" basis.

This indicates that, while much of what must be done revolves
around the trading of variables, a process of "if you will do this, I will
do that" must take place for an acceptable balance to be reached. Such
exchanges are often prompted by "What if…?" questions: this is a specific aspect of negotiation, the process whereby adjustments are made
through making suggestions that offer new ways of rebalancing matters
– "What if I do this, and you then accept (or do) that?" Complex negotiations involve a good deal of this. "What if …?" questions literally
lead the way to successful trading.

But remember that this is not simply a mechanistic process. Rather
it is one strand going on within the total discussion – one utilizing a
variety of techniques and the careful deployment of various behavioural factors (with everything assisted by judicious preparation),
which can make or break your success. Trading must be well executed,
but only as a part of the whole.

With clear objectives and an overall plan in mind, discussions can
proceed. An agenda is sensible for any complex meeting. There is some
merit in being the person to suggest one, albeit describing it as

60 something helpful to both parties. If you say something like: "We might find it best to …", followed by an outline of how you want things to run (though not, of course, saying that this would be helpful to you), this sets the scene. Bear in mind that producing an agenda does have something of a "laying all the cards on the table" feel to it, so you may want to judge its precision and comprehensiveness carefully to allow you some flexibility. Alternatively, it may take on a more demanding tone.

Two key rules

However significant a trade, two important overall rules should always be followed:

RULE 1: Never give a concession for nothing; trade it reluctantly

The first part (never give) is important, because the number of variables is finite and you want your share. The second is too, because perception is as important as fact to how things go. You want to be seen to be driving a hard bargain, otherwise you may not be taken seriously; indeed, any apparent weakness will be pounced on. Remember the saying: if you look like a doormat, people will walk all over you.

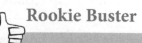

Rookie Buster

If you look like a doormat, people will walk all over you.

RULE 2: Optimize or minimize every concession

This means optimizing your own concessions – talking up their value – and minimizing the value of what you are offered, both while they are discussed and at and after their acceptance. You can do this in terms of both value and how you talk about them. Try to build up the value, significance and importance of anything you offer, and minimize that of what is offered to you. It is not just making or accepting a concession that is important, it is precisely how it is done.

The two sides of this process are worth exploring.

Optimizing your concessions

This means:

- Stressing the cost (financial or otherwise) to you. "Well, I suppose I could do that, but it will involve me in a lot more work."
- Exaggerating, but maintaining credibility. Do not overstate – and, if possible, provide evidence. "Well, I could do that, but it will involve me in at least twice as much work. I have just been through …"
- Referring to a major problem which your concession will solve. "I suppose, if I was to agree that, it would remove the need for you to …"
- Implying that you are making an exceptional concession. "I would never normally do this, but …"

Another approach, suitable for someone you have met before, is:

- Referring to past discussions, and their successful outcome, and what you did for them. "Remember how useful so and so was? I suppose we could go that route again – how about …"

Such lead-ins not only build the significance of what you are offering, and make it more acceptable, but also make it more likely to be accepted quickly, because there is an implied urgency. This is something that you may elect to exaggerate where appropriate.

62   Minimizing their concessions

Even if you plan to accept the concessions, this means:

- Not overdoing the thanks. Not an effusive "Thank you *so* much", but just brief, even dismissive thanks. This is as much a matter of tone as of the actual words used.
- Depreciating them, belittling the value: "Right, that's a small step forward, I guess."
- Amortizing them where appropriate. That is, divide them where possible into smaller units, which will sound less impressive. For example, "Well, at least that would save me £X every month," rather than quoting the annual figure.
- Treating them as given and thus of no real value. A brief acknowledgement may be all that is necessary to give this impression: "Right, let's do it that way."
- Taking it for granted, in fact saying it is not a concession at all but a foregone conclusion: "Fine, I was certainly assuming that …"
- Devaluing by implying you already have what is being offered: "OK, though I already have …"
- Accepting, but in doing so implying that you are doing a favour: "I don't really need that, but fine, let's arrange things that way if you think it helps."
- Linking value to time, implying it is now not worth what is implied: "Well, that helps a little, but it isn't of major importance now you've …"
- Denying any value: "No, that really doesn't help."

Minimizing concessions does not work in every environment. In the Middle East, for instance, the reverse is necessary. Always check local conditions if you have to work overseas, as the local culture will undoubtedly necessitate some fine-tuning of your approach. Indeed, if you negotiate overseas, make sure you understand any cultural differences that may affect your strategy. For instance, you may use a smile with the aim of encouraging agreement, flagging that all is well, but in Korea smiling, especially early in a relationship, is seen as pushy and rude.

Rookie Buster

If you negotiate overseas, make sure you understand any cultural differences that may affect your strategy.

Creating a trading edge

As concessions are either minimized or optimized as appropriate, the skilled negotiator trades a concession which in fact costs them little. It has, though, an implied value which brings a relatively more valuable concession in return from the other side.

It is this difference in value that gives an edge. A concession which you offer, but which you imply is of little or no value, is likely to prompt the offer of a low value concession in return. Thus throughout the process you must play down your thanks for concessions gained and imply their low value, and build up the value of everything that you may concede. The only restraint on this exaggeration is the need to retain credibility with the other person.

It is all a question of degree. The people involved know there is a ritual to the negotiation, but they still have to form a judgement as to how far this goes.

Keeping track

There can be a large number of balls in the air during negotiation. Keeping track of the variables is quite a task, but you can prepare for it. If you have thought through what you want to do, and considered the possibilities and anticipated the reaction of the other side, then you will have a picture that you can amend and adapt as discussions proceed. It may help to imagine the variables as boxes of different weights that can be balanced against each other.

The dangers of not keeping track of the variables are very real. If you forget something, or don't deal with it appropriately and at the

64 right time, it may be impossible to bring it up later, or to do so from a strong position. Make sure you have the overall situation clearly in mind as you deal with the various points. If you make sure you are organized, then anyone less so is at a disadvantage in dealing with you, and this can produce another edge.

Rookie Buster

If you make sure you are organized, then anyone less so is at a disadvantage in dealing with you.

Keeping searching for further variables

You need to remain flexible. Avoid getting locked in to previous plans; remember that planning is only a guide. Good negotiators are quick on their feet. Sometimes what happens is very much along the lines you expect, but some fine tuning is always necessary and sometimes a great deal of adjustment may need to be done. Remember: the saying that "everything is negotiable" can often be true.

Certainly something that has previously been described as fixed may suddenly come into play. There is merit in remaining open minded to such possibilities and, where appropriate, taking the initiative.

Coach's notes

Using and trading with variables is fundamental to successful negotiation. You must:

- Identify all the possible variables ahead of starting a meeting.
- Categorize them and put a priority on them.
- Keep the full list in mind throughout the discussions.
- Trade effectively (using the two rules).
- Keep searching for possible additional variables.
- Manage the process – repeat and note agreements and make and use notes as necessary to help you keep track and stay ahead of the game.

Go for it! Young Annabel, whose strategy for getting a pet guinea pig is quoted in the Introduction, already grasps the basis for all this at the age of 6, so it cannot be too difficult. The problem, if there is one, is the number of variables with which you must juggle. It is easy to get flustered in the heat of the moment and lose track of what you are trying to do; hence the need for sound preparation. But given that and some organization (and some notes), there is no reason why you cannot get to grips with this process quite quickly – and indeed, making an initial trade or two can quickly give you confidence and allow you to move on to more complex negotiations.

Notes

The word "complexity" has appeared alongside "negotiation" several times now, and this chapter makes clear just why that is. Here and in the next chapter we investigate a whole range of factors (approaches, techniques and out-and-out ploys), all of which can contribute to your negotiating success, and show how they can be deployed to strengthen what you do.

CHAPTER 5

Deploying the tactics

A good many detailed tactics are important throughout a meeting as it progresses. These must be deployed carefully, and the precise manner in which this is done may make the difference between striking a deal that is good or merely OK. These factors should be regarded as cumulative in effect. One may help; the right mix may clinch the deal. What is more, the way you deploy such techniques may need to be disguised, or at least not made obvious. As the Duc de la Rochefoucauld said, "The height of cleverness is to be able to conceal it."

Conducting the negotiation

The complexities of negotiation put a high premium on managing the meeting effectively. During the process, two separate factors run in parallel:

- The process and the tactics of negotiation.
- The interpersonal behaviour which accompanies them.

Both are important separately and also in the way that they work

70 together. In order to build up a clear picture of the process, we will leave the question of interpersonal behaviour on one side until later (Chapter 7) and deal specifically with the tactical basis for negotiation.

Using variables: the fundamentals

As we have seen, a good knowledge of all the variables, and their possible use in trading, is key. You need to:

- See variables in the round in order to prepare an opening strategy – a starting point for discussion.
- Decide how the variables can be used to trade. And assess their respective worth.
- Continue to search throughout the negotiation for additional factors that might be used as variables.

Occasionally, one party in negotiation holds all the cards and the result may be in little doubt. More often, though, the situation is not a foregone conclusion. The balance might go either way, and things start apparently on a flat field, but many arrangements are possible. Alongside the core trading, the techniques of how exactly things are done can come into their own. The techniques of negotiation must be selected and deployed to strengthen what you do and enhance the deal you agree.

Rookie Buster

The techniques of negotiation must be selected and deployed to strengthen what you do and enhance the deal you agree.

Using power in negotiation

What swings the balance? It is the power to negotiate that both sides bring to the table. Everyone hopes to have the balance of power. It is something to consider in your planning and certainly something to be realistic about; a major mistake made by some negotiators is to over (or under) estimate the power held by either themselves or their opposite number.

The word "power" is used here in a very specific manner. Negotiators mean a number of things by it. The main power factors are:

- *Using specific variables.* The most obvious sources of power are the specific variables that are most important to a particular negotiation. These can be almost anything, from major matters such as financial arrangements, including price, discounts and payment terms, to a plethora of others. They can be either tangible or intangible, and usually both are involved. This is an area where feeling is as important as substance. For instance, aspects of the example of the annual general meeting mentioned earlier may well be subjective: how will the way it is organized affect the participants, for instance?

- *Using a promise of reward.* This term describes something you can offer that the other party definitely wants, and acts to ensure that they listen. The banquet manager in the AGM example wants the business, giving one major element of power to the meeting organizer. There is also a corresponding negative side to this ...

- *Using a threat of punishment.* This is where there is an apparent intention *not* to give something that the other party wants. Thus, if the banquet manager refuses to agree some factor important to the organizer, he wields power; this may be increased if the organizer knows it is short notice and he is unlikely to get availability and a better deal elsewhere.

- *Using legitimacy.* Legitimacy means the factual evidence. It can swing the balance without much

72 argument: for example, if the event organizer shows a written quote for a lower price from another venue then, provided it compares like with like, its presence influences both parties. What is important, though, is that it *seems* to compare like with like; after all, there is a degree of deviousness about negotiation.

- *Using bogeys.* Bogeys are factors used specifically to produce an edge. They may not stand up to close examination, but in the throes of a meeting can be used to good effect. For example, saying, "My chairman is insistent upon ..." may succeed in labelling a particular point as unalterable, while the truth of the matter may remain hidden and unexplored (and may be different). Bogeys may be factors used only for what they can achieve, or may be factors that are actually of some importance, but which are given artificial weight in the hope of their securing an edge.

- *Showing confidence.* Confidence comes in part from preparation. It has a lot to do with the human and behavioural aspects of negotiation, which are explored in depth later. It is harder to deal with someone who appears very confident, and who seems to have every reason to be so. Clearly, you want to feel that the one with the most justifiable confidence is you, and you should work in every way possible to achieve this.

The power a negotiator assembles and deploys, and how that is seen by the other party, creates the foundation from which techniques in turn can be deployed, and allows the negotiation to be directed towards chosen objectives.

Rookie Buster

It is harder to deal with someone who appears very confident, and who seems to have every reason to be so.

As you think through what the bargaining variables are, try to   73
assess the power they give you. This is not simply a numbers game.
Having a larger number of variables, while undeniably useful, may not
of itself guarantee more negotiating power. Some variables may be
lightweight and make little difference; others may be particularly
telling and powerful.

Focusing on the key principles

There are four vital overall guiding principles which combine to help
the successful management of negotiations:
- Set your sights high.
- Find out the other person's full intentions.
- Keep all of the factors in mind.
- Keep looking for further variables.

These four guiding principles can put you ahead of the game;
remembering these principles is perhaps the most important step
towards maximizing your negotiating expertise.

Rookie Buster

Remembering these principles is perhaps the most
important step towards maximizing your negotiating
expertise.

These are so important that they deserve some comment about
each.

74 Set your sights high

"Faint heart never won fair lady," goes an old saying. Always aim high. It is important to aim for the top, for the best deal you can imagine, because it is always easier to manage the process from this starting point. Aim high: you can always trade down; indeed you may often have to do so, but it is more difficult to trade up having stated your intentions.

Rookie Buster

Aim high: you can always trade down.

It is especially difficult to change tactics and trade up once you are into the meeting. It is for this reason that having a clear view of the variables (the must-haves, etc., detailed at the start of Chapter 4) is so useful. You may not always achieve exactly what you want, but the chances of getting close are most likely with this approach.

Find out the other person's full intentions

Think of the other person in the same way as you think of yourself. They too have a shopping list of what they want to do. The better your information about what this is, the better you will be able to operate. Success may relate directly to how much you know about the other person's shopping list; it pays to find out as much as you can.

Rookie Buster

Success may relate directly to how much you know about the other person's shopping list; it pays to find out as much as you can.

It is easy to make superficial judgements. There may well be some obvious things the other side are after, but other factors matter too, as do their priorities. The more complete your picture the better. Information may come from:

- Prior preparation.
- Knowledge or experience of the person or situation, or others like them.
- Questions asked as an integral, perhaps early, part of the negotiation meeting.

Infer sensibly by all means, but be wary of making unwarranted assumptions during the meeting as this can lead you on false trails if you are wrong. It is all too easy to come out of a meeting that has not gone so well, saying "But it all seemed so obvious ..." Your thinking so may have been the exact intention of your adversary. Remember the old saying: Never ass/u/me anything – it makes an ass out of you and me.

Rookie Buster

Never ass/u/me anything – it makes an ass out of you and me.

76 Keep all of the factors in mind

As the picture builds up, the complexities grow. It is easy as you plan ahead to forget some of the issues you need to keep in mind. You need to keep a clear head, to make notes, to think and recap as necessary if each step forward is going to work.

Keep looking for further variables

This must be something that continues through-out. Variables may be many and varied. Any of them may play an important part in the process. Sometimes changing circumstances and perspectives as a negotiation proceeds allow a variable to be used in a way that did not seem possible earlier on; and this may be true even after something has apparently been ruled out or declared "fixed". Seeking for opportunities amongst variables should never cease.

Managing the process

The process of negotiation is based on what is called a point of balance. It is inherent in the process that while participants start far apart on the scale of possibilities for agreement, they will settle on something they can both relate to as a reasonable deal. The point of balance on which agreement is struck is not, of course, usually spot on the centre. A range of solutions is possible around the middle point. Similarly the furthest or most extreme points from the centre are usually quickly recognized by both parties as unrealistic goals and only relevant as starting points. Movement along the scale is what defines a discussion as a negotiation.

Acknowledging the history of contact

Negotiation rarely comes out of the blue. There is usually a history of contact between the two parties, which may include written contact such as correspondence, or earlier meetings. Whether extensive or minimal, such initial communication sets the scene and to some extent provides the agenda. This is often seen in wage bargaining. The employees ask for 8 per cent, the employer snorts with derision and offers 3 per cent, and everyone knows that settlement will be somewhere in between (though not necessarily exactly halfway, of course).

Negotiation needs an agenda. It may be useful to recap, to refer to the case so far, to any agreements made or indications given, or to whatever history may be useful or necessary. Persuasion precedes negotiation, so if during first contacts you were concerned with a more fundamental agreement, and a case had to be accepted before terms and conditions could be debated, then this too may need to be referred to.

The initial stance

This refers to the point that each party starts from. Start as you mean to go on; a good start gives you confidence and can put the other side on to the wrong foot early on.

Rookie Buster

Start as you mean to go on; a good start gives you confidence and can put the other side on to the wrong foot early on.

Some judgement is necessary in choosing your initial stance, as the right starting point can facilitate the moves you want to make thereafter. There are many options – for instance:

- *Going for the quick kill.* At one end of the scale you can go for what is described as the quick kill – "Here are my conditions, take them or leave them." Such an approach does not, in fact, rule out negotiation. It simply starts by making it clear a hard line is being taken and little will be given away. Working from a powerful position, this or something close to it may be an appropriate starting point. (Such a position is often used in wage bargaining.) But even though it implies strength it must allow for some change or it risks being rejected out of hand. The ritual is important, and if people expect some movement this approach may stretch their credulity.
- *Taking a softer approach.* At the other end of the scale, or towards it, the conversation might start on a different note, something like: "Let's talk about what you want." This implies that you are reasonable people and want to secure agreement. This may be more suitable when you do not have such a clearly strong case, but go too far with it and it will create, or increase, disadvantage.

It is sometimes said that the higher the opening bid (or initial stance), the better the final deal achieved by whoever makes it. Certainly it is difficult to negotiate down from nothing, and an initially exaggerated stance can throw the other party off balance and change their perception about the kind of deal that might be struck. This can mean that the first phase of negotiation is only a clarification of initial stances. A better, less extreme, point is then adopted by each party. Then negotiation really gets under way.

Building bridges to agreement

Consider what is going on as the negotiation commences. On the one hand taking initial stances distances participants, like two knights taking up positions on opposite hill tops prior to meeting to do battle in the valley between.

On the other hand, and because of this, there is a need to build what are called "bridges of rapport". These are inserted to bring the parties together, or at least somewhat closer, in a way that prompts discussion and sets the scene for what needs to be achieved. Each party will introduce bridges that help their own case.

The other party is more likely to see your point of view if they can relate to your position and circumstance. Bridges make this more likely. There are many approaches, for example:

- Open the discussions on a neutral subject, to allay any hostility, obtain some initial agreement and get the other person talking.
- When holding back, give assurance that you will make every effort to come to a mutually agreeable outcome.
- Demonstrate respect for both the other party and the process you are embarking on. For example, compliment them about something already done that helps the process.
- Refer back to past agreement. This reinforces persuasion.
- Present some of the values in your offering, even if you plan to negotiate them out later.
- Be clear about complex issues.

All such tactics put the conversation on a basis of sweet reason. Even attempts to get the other party's list of requirements on the table can be undertaken in a way that seems helpful: take an interest in them, their needs and views. This combines a show of genuine concern with something that, in fact, strengthens your position.

Keeping finding out

Ask questions, and listen – really listen – to the answers. Keep the other party's position clearly in mind. Information is power in negotiation, and while you do not want to make people feel they are undergoing the Spanish Inquisition, the more you discover the better. Try to strike the right balance.

Asking questions may seem sensible enough, but questioning is more than just blurting out the first thing that comes to mind – "Why do you say that?" Even a simple phrase may carry overtones and people wonder if you are suggesting they should not have said that, or if you see no relevance for the point made. In addition, many questions can easily be ambiguous. It is all too easy to ask something that, only because it is loosely phrased, prompts an unintended response. Ask "How long will that take?" and the reply may simply be "Not long." Ask "Will you finish that before the meeting scheduled for 11 o'clock on Wednesday?" and you are much more likely to be able to decide exactly what to do when you have a clear answer.

Beyond simple clarity you need to consider and use three distinctly different kinds of question:

1. **Closed questions**. These prompt rapid "Yes" or "No" answers, and are useful both as a starting point (they can also be made easy to answer to help ease someone into the questioning process) and to gain rapid confirmation of something. Too many closed questions, on the other hand, create a virtual monologue in which the questioner seems to be doing most of the talking, and this can be annoying or unsatisfying to the other person.

2. **Open questions**. These are questions phrased so that they cannot be answered with a simple "Yes" or "No" and typically begin with words like "what", "where", "why", "how", "who" and "when", and phrases such as "Tell me about …" Such questions get people talking, so that they feel involved and they like the tone of the conversation. By prompting a fuller answer and encouraging people to explain, open questions also produce far more information than closed questions.

3. **Probing questions**. These are a series of linked questions designed to pursue a point: thus a second question such as

"What else is important about …" or a phrase like "Tell me more about …" gets people to fill out a picture, and can thus produce both more detail and expose the "why" which lies behind more superficial answers.

Many a communication is made to succeed by the simple prerequisite of starting it with some questions; so too with negotiating.

Go for it! Let us end this chapter by returning to the four central factors mentioned earlier:

- Set your sights high.
- Find out the other person's full intentions.
- Keep all of the factors in mind.
- Keep looking for further variables.

You will find that utilizing these principles really can take negotiating to the next level; insistence on these will go a long way towards making you seem professional and also towards making your negotiating work effectively.

Notes

84

Keeping in mind the range of core techniques described in the last chapter, this chapter reviews some additional techniques that can make your negotiating work effectively. Here are ten key ideas to add to your armoury and enhance your basic negotiating skills.

CHAPTER 6

Further techniques to keep you ahead

Ten top tactics

The techniques that follow can be used, together or separately, as appropriate. While you need to be aware of the danger of adding too much to the mix and making things overcomplicated, these techniques can all help, and neglecting one when it would be effective can risk your hopes of success. You need to be prepared to use each or all of the available techniques as appropriate to maximize your negotiating skill.

1. Use silence
Saying nothing can sometimes be as powerful as speaking, provided that silence is used at the right time and in the right way. As most people quickly feel embarrassed by a silence, after even a few seconds, it can take a conscious effort to hold it, but it can be worthwhile, so:

- In trading concessions, if you cannot optimize or minimize, silence can imply that you are non-committal.
- Being silent can imply certainty on your part, and thus uncertainty for the other party. Having made a clear suggestion, you wait. You will find it's not so difficult to ensure the other

86 person speaks first. Maybe they need to think about it. If you chip in prematurely, you may find yourself diluting your case unnecessarily.

Here is an example of using silence. A company buyer is speaking on the telephone to a potential supplier and, with a good quote in front of him, challenges the price, but without really saying anything about it: "I am still a bit concerned about the price." The supplier defends the deal as being good, which it is. He asks the buyer if it does not seem reasonable; the buyer says nothing at all. Embarrassed, the supplier starts to justify the figures and again ends with a question that is ignored. After three silences, which the supplier finds awkward, he says: "Would another five per cent off get the order?" And the deal is done!

A silence can be powerful. It can be better than asking questions, and is always a hard argument to counter. The need to fill the silence can result in your learning more, as thoughts are expressed for no better reason than to fill the gap. If your questions are not coped with well by the other party, it is an easy technique with which to win points. Remember the saying: Talk less, learn more. In negotiating this can not only help, but it can also be a powerful technique.

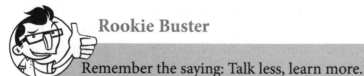

Rookie Buster

Remember the saying: Talk less, learn more.

2. Summarize frequently

By definition, negotiations can often be complex. They involve juggling a number of variables. It is easy to lose the thread. Never be afraid to summarize: recap where you have got to so far and how one aspect of the discussion has been left. Linking this to the words "suppose" or "if" keeps the conversation organized and allows you to explore possibilities without committing yourself until you are ready. You might make this sort of comment: "Right, you have agreed that you need to sort out cost, delivery and timing. Now if you take …, then …" Keep tabs on the exact state of play throughout the process; being organized and on top of things in this way can give you an edge, especially over a less organized opponent. This goes hand in hand with the next point.

Rookie Buster

Keep tabs on the exact state of play throughout the process; being organized and on top of things in this way can give you an edge, especially over a less organized opponent.

3. Make notes

This too helps to keep complex negotiations on track. While certain meetings are too informal for full note-taking to be appropriate, even a few words noted down can help. Information is power, especially when you have more pertinent information than the other party.

Rookie Buster

Information is power, especially when you have more pertinent information than the other party.

Never find yourself having to ask what was said. Not only will the lack of recall worry you, but the fact that you need to ask calls your expertise into question and may spur the other party on to try harder. Taking notes will not only prevent you being caught out over something factual, but making or checking them can have another advantage: it gives you time to think. As you say "Let me just note that down,"

88 or as you check ("Let me just see what we agreed about that"), you can be thinking. The brain works faster than the pen. It is surprising how much thinking you can do as you write two or three (sometimes irrelevant!) words on your pad.

4. Leave people feeling each step is good

Negotiation typically builds agreement progressively. Make sure you emphasize that each stage is good – preferably in a way that stresses this for both parties, but particularly for the other party – as you proceed. Phrases like "That's a good arrangement," "That will work well," "That's fair," or "That's a good suggestion" help build the agreement. Making people feel that everything is progressing well for them helps maintain a positive and constructive feeling to the meeting.

Rookie Buster

Making people feel that everything is progressing well for them helps maintain a positive and constructive feeling to the meeting.

5. Read between the lines

Remember that negotiation is essentially an adversarial process. Both parties want the best for themselves, and the only signs of any approaching traps come via the other person, as do signs of success around the corner. You should watch particularly for danger phrases that often mean something other than they seem – sometimes even the very opposite. For example:

- "You're a reasonable fellow." (Actually means: "Look how reasonable I am.")
- "That's much fairer for both of us." (Actually means: "Especially for me.")
- "It looks like you are about there." (Actually means: "There is something else I want.")

- "All that's left is to sort out a couple of minor details." (Actually
  means: "They may be minor for you, but not for me…")
- "That's all, then." (Which will inevitably be followed by: "Actually,
  there is just one more thing …")

Listening is therefore as important to the negotiator as speaking. We return to this concept later. Read the other person accurately, make it clear that you are doing so, and you will cramp their style in terms of possible future ploys.

Rookie Buster

Read the other person accurately, make it clear that you are doing so, and you will cramp their style in terms of possible future ploys.

6. Remain neutral

Maintain neutrality as much and as long as possible. Negotiation works best as a balancing exercise. If you throw the whole basis of discussion up in the air – "It is not as good as the other deal I am considering" – you risk taking everything back to square one, quite possibly enough to make it necessary to switch back to persuasion mode. You may in fact *want* to go back if you are not happy with the offer or the terms and conditions. But if you do, you risk drawing out the whole process; this may be worthwhile, but equally it may cause problems, and you need to be aware of this. Keeping everything businesslike and professional – using a seemingly dispassionate approach and style – tends to work best in terms of the end result.

Rookie Buster

Keeping everything businesslike and professional –
using a seemingly dispassionate approach and style –
tends to work best in terms of the end result.

7. Concentrate all the time

Concentrate. Build in time to think if necessary. The power of silence
has been mentioned; use it to think ahead. Use any delaying tactic to
stop you getting into difficulty, and always engage the brain before the
mouth. Use a calculator, make a telephone call or just say "Let me
think about that for a moment," but give yourself pause for thought.
Preparation and practice both make concentration easier, the first
because you know what to concentrate on, and the second because you
learn how important it is.

Rookie Buster

Preparation and practice both make concentration
easier, the first because you know what to concentrate on,
and the second because you learn how important it is.

On the other hand, if you can make the other party leap before they
look, so much the better.

8. Keep your powder dry

Beware of acting precipitately. Try not to make an offer, certainly not
a final offer, until everything that needs negotiating is on the table.
This may need no more than a question: "Yes, I am sure I can help
there, but is there anything else you want to consider?" You may need
to probe to be sure of your ground before you proceed. Never close

off your options until you have to; this is good advice for the   91
negotiator.

Rookie Buster

Never close off your options until you have to.

9. Beware of deadlines

It is said that there has never been a deadline in history that was not negotiable. Timing is a variable. How long will things take? When will they happen? One at a time? All at once? Keep this in mind at all stages of the process. Remember too that most people build in ample contingency. When someone says something must be done by a particular date, their absolute deadline is almost certainly later. Remember too that a missed deadline, perhaps long after a negotiation has taken place, is always noticed and resented; it can sour future transactions.

Rookie Buster

Remember that a missed deadline, perhaps long after a negotiation has taken place, is always noticed and resented.

10. Remember that constraints and variables are interchangeable

Almost anything the other side presents as fixed may be made into a variable. The word "fixed" is as likely to mean that someone does not *want* to negotiate this, as that they are *unwilling* or *unable* to use it as a variable. It pays to act accordingly. As soon as you hear the word "fixed", ask yourself – does it actually mean fixed, or something else? Very often challenging this will score you points.

92

Rookie Buster

As soon as you hear the word "fixed", ask yourself – does it actually mean fixed, or something else?

Your way

None of these points is complex in itself. They all illustrate the multi-faceted nature of negotiation, in which a great deal is going on. Such techniques are useful; but none is a cure-all that will single-handedly ensure you conclude the deal you want. The trick is in the overall orchestration of what you do. Regard every negotiation meeting as *yours*. Because of the need to orchestrate a complex process, it helps if you are in the driving seat. A line from Shakespeare's *Much Ado About Nothing* puts it well, saying that if "two men ride of a horse, one must ride behind". Meetings, too, need someone in front, taking the lead. Taking a leading role does not necessarily mean being heavy-handed, and indeed it may not even be obvious who is running things. Run the conversation that you want, in a way that they find they like, or at least find acceptable or professional.

Rookie Buster

Run the conversation that you want, in a way that they find they like, or at least find acceptable or professional.

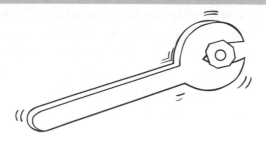

Getting off to a good start sets the process in train. Fine-tuning as you go along keeps you progressing matters as you want, towards your goals and along the lines of your plan. This means you need to be extra conscious of what the other person appears to be up to, and of how the interpersonal behaviour of the transaction is likely to work – a topic reviewed in the next chapter.

The benefits of a careful approach

With all these techniques to consider, let's not forget that the overall process is important too. Look at this example: Linda and Harry are due to meet a surveyor, Sue, from their local council. They need planning permission before they can expand their current site and implement expansion plans for their business.

The matter is complex. There are matters of access, parking and congestion, employment and building regulation. They envisage a long discussion.

Linda and Harry discuss the matter ahead of the meeting and lay out a strategy. Because of the complexity, they arrange a logical order for the discussion and consider how to persuade Sue to accept it. They divide their task between the two of them; one will lead on some points, the other on others. This is primarily to keep things manageable. Though it is important for both to be involved in the discussion, Linda has the smaller proportion of the tasks. Because of this, one of her tasks is to keep a note of the balance. She will be the note-taker. Having the best view of how things stand at any particular moment, she will be responsible for keeping the two of them on track during discussions, which will inevitably get more confusing as they progress.

The thinking described above makes good sense. Maintaining a vision of the broad picture as you proceed is as important as the tactics deployed at a particular moment to settle an issue. Note that when more than one person on each side is involved in discussions, the team itself becomes a key factor in securing an edge. In good teamwork one and one makes more than two! The way people work together should

94 appear seamless, and can add considerable strength to a situation if this is deployed as an active ingredient and made to work well.

 **Rookie Buster**

In good teamwork one and one makes more than two!

Coach's notes

There is lots to think about here, but let's summarize the process at this stage. You should:

- Be sure you know what gives you (and them) power.
- Keep the process manageable: focus on the key operational process of negotiation, such as setting your sights high.
- Plan to make a good start.
- Deal effectively with the trading that forms the core of negotiation.
- Know the techniques, and when and how to use them.

Go for it! There are many skills that demand considerable breadth of thinking. The mind must seemingly focus on an impossible variety of disparate things. Just how do people (well, some people, anyway) manage to juggle with flaming torches without burning holes in the carpet? But they do, even if the fire brigade does get called out a few times in the earlier stages. The danger here is that, as you begin to understand just how many things need to be kept in mind while negotiating, you may find it overwhelming.

Don't panic, though. Practice makes perfect. Things do come together, and the trick is simply not to bite off more than you can chew. Think about what you want to do, introduce techniques progressively and allow habits to form that will make the process easier. It is possible. You will do it. If it helps, think of some of the losers in your organization who seem to cope! If they can do it, so can you.

Notes

In addition to the tangible techniques reviewed to date, there is another dimension that influences negotiation, that of the interpersonal behaviour that colours, indeed influences, the meeting. You need to keep an eye on this too, watching what is being done to you, and planning your own behaviour to aid your intentions. This chapter sets out the key principles that will allow you to operate successfully on this level and thus put together a strong overall approach.

CHAPTER 7

Adding another dimension

Using interpersonal behaviour

Negotiation is not simply a matter of techniques, important though these are. It also depends on reading the behaviour of the other people involved, and using behaviour appropriately yourself. Reading between the lines and acting accordingly is part of the negotiating ritual. To a degree, fluency in this is a matter of experience, which you will build up over time. Nevertheless, certain principles can be useful.

This section looks at the key behavioural aspects of:

- Reading between the lines.
- Listening.
- Questioning.
- Non-verbal signals (body language).

So, let's consider these in turn.

100 *Reading verbal signs*

Negotiation has a language of its own. Some of it becomes ritual, adding nothing to persuasiveness, and functioning simply as a part of the fabric rather than being significant for the content of what is being said. Some is a ploy, and you need to be able to read between the lines to see what motivation lies behind a particular comment or phrase.

We are all familiar with a number of phrases that in general should simply not be believed. These may include: "Trust me," "I only say this for your own good," and the classic, "The cheque is in the post." Here, however, the complexities are greater, and it is hidden meanings we are after. For instance, consider the hidden signals in the following examples, with the possible subtext shown in brackets:

- "We would find it extremely difficult to meet the deadline." (*Unspoken meaning*: "If we do meet it, it must be worth something.")
- "Our organization is not set up to cope with that." (*Unspoken meaning*: "So if we do, consider it a significant favour.")
- "I do not have the authority to arrange …" (*Unspoken meaning*: "… but someone else has.")
- "It is not our normal practice to do that." (*Unspoken meaning*: "But I could make an exception.")
- "I never negotiate on price." (*Unspoken meaning*: "If you want to – you start.")
- "We can discuss that point." (*Unspoken meaning*: "It is negotiable.")
- "We are not prepared to discuss that at this stage." (*Unspoken meaning*: "But we will later.")
- "That's very much more than our budget." (*Unspoken meaning*: "So it had better add real value and extra benefits.")
- "It is not our policy to give additional discounts, and if we did they would not be as much as ten per cent." (*Unspoken meaning*: "Would you accept five?")
- "Our price for that quantity is X." (*Unspoken meaning*: "But for larger quantities …")
- "Those are the standard terms and conditions." (*Unspoken*

meaning: "And I hope I don't have to vary them, but I will if I must.")

- "It seems an extremely reasonable arrangement." (*Unspoken meaning*: "It is best for me.")
- "It is a good price." (*Unspoken meaning*: "It's profitable for us.")
- "I can't say I am happy with the arrangement but ..." (*Unspoken meaning*: "I agree that, but may ask for something else to balance it.")

You will no doubt come across – and may yourself use in future – many more. The detail and the nuances of everything said when negotiating are very important. Does what is said mean exactly what it seems? Can you check? Is it a ploy? Is it an opportunity? How can you gain an edge with a word or phrase? Keep your ears open and be vigilant; it is wise to be constantly watchful, to take nothing at face value.

Rookie Buster

Keep your ears open and be vigilant; it is wise to be constantly watchful, to take nothing at face value.

Remember that when you use phrases with nuances, they help you; but if the other party uses similar things, they may provide warning signs, or potentially take you in a direction that puts you at a disadvantage. Recognizing them, and their potential danger, is the first step to overcoming them if they are deployed against you.

Using behavioural techniques

The following are all good and common examples of the almost limitless behavioural factors that can play a part in negotiation discussions.

102 Keeping the temperature under control

You negotiate best with a calm, considered approach. So does the other person. Whilst you do not want to make it easy for them, you do not want the fabric of negotiation to collapse either. Any behaviour you use must help your cause without demolishing the process.

Rookie Buster

Any behaviour you use must help your cause without demolishing the process.

It is easy to get into a position where pursuing your cause does more harm than good. For instance, if you labour an issue on which agreement is difficult and refuse to budge, particularly early on in a discussion, you may create an impasse from which it is difficult for either party to retreat. You need to keep the range of issues in mind. If necessary you might leave a point on one side to return to later. Having agreed some of the issues, overall views change. At a stage where a deal seems very possible, an early sticking point may not seem so important and can then be resolved without real difficulty.

Using hidden motives

Icebergs are a danger to shipping not so much because of what can be seen, but because most of their volume cannot be seen; it is hidden below the surface. The iceberg concept can apply to discussion and negotiation. You ask something and do not seem to get a straight answer. The other party's suspicion may prevent it; they are so busy looking for hidden motives that they hinder agreement for no good reason.

It may make sense to spell out why you are doing things, asking a certain question – "If you can tell me …, then I …." – or pursuing a certain line, so that at least most of what is hidden becomes clear. Of course, you may have motives you want to keep hidden, at least for the moment, but it will not help if the other person thinks you are being several times more devious than you are.

Flagging

Clear flagging or signposting – that is, spelling out how you are proceeding – can help. Sometimes it just makes clear what you are doing: "May I ask …?" Or "Perhaps I might suggest …?" At other times a specific reason makes getting what you want more likely: "I think it might be easier to settle other details if you can agree a fixed budget first." This can be seen as a constructive step forward.

On the other hand, you should never flag disagreement. This is something to watch, as the natural response is to flag it instantly. Consider what happens in a simple example about encouraging constructive listening:

A makes a suggestion: "Perhaps we can aim for completion of stage one by Friday week." B immediately disagrees: "No, I think that's far too late." Even if B goes on to explain why, and even if he is right, A is busy developing a retaliatory response from the moment he hears the word "no". A does not listen to the explanation of why, and even if it is half heard, he is already committed to a riposte.

People are more likely to listen constructively and accept reasons if they are given *before* disagreement is flagged.

Rookie Buster

People are more likely to listen constructively and accept reasons if they are given *before* disagreement is flagged.

Thus, when A makes his point, B could respond, initially seeming to agree: "That would be good. However, you agreed that the whole project should be finished by the end of the month. Does Friday week leave sufficient time for everything else?" Alternatively A might precede their suggestion with a reason. Either approach will be more likely to prompt thought and discussion, and thus allow a compromise to be found or a counter-suggestion to be accepted.

Summarizing progress

Good negotiators summarize regularly; many negotiations get complex and discussions can last a while. So summarizing can:

- Test progress and allow you to rephrase things said by the other party.
- Help you gain the initiative in the discussion, or maintain the dialogue.
- Ensure that both parties have similar interpretations of what is said, and thus avoid misunderstanding and subsequent acrimony.

If you adopt the role of undertaking to summarize regularly, it will not only help keep the discussion on track, it will also help put you in the driving seat and influence how you are seen.

Attacking psychologically 105

Some things are said, not as a tangible part of any argument, but to put the other party at a psychological disadvantage: to rattle them. Some comments of this kind may be based on issues which are part of the discussion, such as pressure on timing and deadlines. Others may be purely cosmetic, like a (contrived) interruption, or a pause to make an urgent telephone call. They create a long silence or pause in the discussion, during which the instigator can be thinking and the other party is sweating. All sorts of things can be used in this way, amongst them:

- Playing for time: working something out on a calculator or making a phone call.
- An irrelevant digression.
- A smoke screen of demands, only one of which is important.
- Flattery or coercion.
- An angry outburst or show of emotion.
- Apparent total fluency with the facts; wondrous mental arithmetic may have been worked out beforehand, or could be just be guesswork, but said with sufficient authority to sound definitive.
- Physical arrangements: an uncomfortable chair or position (such as balancing a coffee cup while trying to take notes).
- Financial restraints made to seem irreversible.
- Pretended misunderstanding.

Avoiding defence/attack spirals

Because people instinctively feel it is not proper to attack someone without warning, disagreement often starts from mild beginnings. Whilst one party says they are not sure about something, or that they think they should aim for better than that, gently moving towards a major negative, the other senses what is happening and begins to prepare a counter-argument.

Good negotiators do not put the other party on their guard, as doing so effectively provides time for them to react well. If it is appropriate to attack, then do so firmly, at once and without warning.

Rookie Buster

If it is appropriate to attack, then do so firmly, at once and without warning.

Proposing counter-suggestions

Suppose you make proposal X and then the other person makes proposal Y. If you automatically think the other person is disagreeing, you will not be receptive and may not consider the alternative properly. If this happens, your riposte can lead into a series of monologues, with each side seeing the other as unhelpful and unconstructive. This means that progress is blocked, even if proposal X and Y are not really so far apart, and things could be coming together. Avoiding this danger needs careful judgement.

Avoiding deadlock

The purpose of negotiation is to make a deal. Deadlock does nothing for either party. The search for variables has to go on until a mutually acceptable deal is possible. It is usually only a question of time. However, if there are moments of deadlock, it is helpful to think of the conversation flowing like a stream, which will always find a path around obstructions rather than through them.

Never underestimate the chances of a new path, nor overestimate your opponent's power and determination to remain unmoving. Try to find out why there is deadlock, and search widely for concessions or variables that will break it. In dire cases suggest a break, agreeing as much as possible before it, or even adding in the involvement of other people. Try anything to create a real shift in what is happening.

Using ritual approaches

In certain parts of the world it is necessary to bargain in the shops and markets, not simply to secure a good price, but to win respect. The process itself is important, not just the outcome.

This is true of any negotiating situation. Some professional negotiators, who enjoy the game, feel frustrated if agreement is too quick or too simple. Certainly negotiation must be allowed to take its course, and some people will put up more and more conditions or elements to keep the process going. In such circumstances it may be wise never to make the first offer, and not to make unacceptable conditions or drive impossible bargains.

An example of this also makes a point about international differences. A man visiting Hong Kong for the first time wishes to buy a watch. He has been told about the bargaining, and the percentage drop in price for which he should aim. He sets off round the shops and, despite his best efforts, gets only halfway towards the planned discount. Back at his hotel, discussing this with a local colleague, he asks what it was that he was doing wrong. "How long were you in each shop?" asks the colleague. On hearing that it was ten minutes or so, he suggests that the visitor tries again, but gives it half an hour.

The newcomer then discovers that only after twenty minutes or so, when you're sitting on a stool and tea has been produced, does the bargaining get serious. This time he comes out with a nice watch and a good deal, and a little more understanding about the psychology of negotiation and the way things can work in a different culture.

There are limits, of course, but if the other party wants to take their time, let them. It may be worth it in the end. Timing is an important factor, and has to be handled just right (you can get into trouble if you are in effect a time waster). Do not underestimate what is going on at a psychological level; doing so can put you at serious disadvantage.

Rookie Buster

Do not underestimate what is going on at a psychological level; doing so can put you at serious disadvantage.

Linking to future relationships

Always aim to end on a pleasant note. Negotiation can get acrimonious, hard bargains are driven, but people may well need to work or play together again. It may be good for future relations for the last move to be towards the other party, maybe throwing in one last small sweetener as the final agreement is made. This can stand you in good stead next time round. Negotiating with colleagues may be a regular part of your work, and you do not want one resounding win to affect every future exchange.

Listening better

Many problems of communication are due to people not listening. Listening is always important, especially in a complex interaction such as negotiation. It is easy to be distracted, and you need to concentrate. Daydreaming, however constructively, is all too easy. Give the other party your undivided attention.

Another distraction is emotion. As the other person's argument unfolds, you perhaps begin to feel anxious, or become angry; and if such resentment takes over and prevents you listening, then your case will suffer. You may want to keep your first reactions hidden. It can be difficult to refer back to something later saying that it is a minor difficulty if at the time when it was raised your face registered total dismay.

Check you have heard correctly 109

Never be afraid to interrupt a long speech to double-check you are following it. Ask for simplification or repetition if you wish. Beware too of hearing what you want to hear. Do not make assumptions; act on what the true message is. You may need to analyse the message as it proceeds and begin to form a response, but you have to keep listening as you do so if you are not to run into problems. Remember, one missed point can not only cause a momentary hiatus, but – if undiscovered – may also leave you labouring under a misapprehension throughout the rest of the meeting.

Rookie Buster

Never be afraid to interrupt a long speech to double-check you are following it.

Making listening easier

In addition, think about what will make listening easier. You cannot concentrate on what is being said if there is a lot of background noise, for example in an open-plan office, or if you are busy with something else as you talk, such as driving a car. Try to pick a time when you are at your best, not over-tired or distracted by some personal emergency. The next section adds to what may seem obvious, but shows how you can maximize the effect.

Attention, please!

Do not look back, but can you remember the two words in the main heading leading into the topic of listening? If not (and be honest), then think about it – if we are not fully concentrating, we do not take in

110 every detail of what we are reading or hearing. (The heading read "Listening better" – but equally it could have been "Listening elephants", on the basis that whatever their hearing might be like, elephants have big ears and good memories!)

The key thing then is to regard listening as an *active* process. It is something we all need to work at. What does this mean? There is perhaps a surprising number of ways in which we can focus and improve both our listening and the retention of information, including details crucial to understanding, that good listening enables. These include the need to:

- Want to listen: this is easy once you realize how useful it is to the communication process.
- Look like a good listener: people will appreciate it, and if they see they have your attention and feedback they will be more forthcoming.
- Understand: it is not just the words, but the meaning that lies behind them that you must note.
- React: let people see that you have heard and understood and are interested. Nods, small gestures and signs and comments will encourage the other person's confidence and participation.
- Stop talking: other than small acknowledgements, you cannot talk and listen at the same time. Do not interrupt.
- Use empathy: put yourself in the other person's shoes and make sure you really appreciate their point of view.
- Check: if necessary, ask questions promptly to clarify matters as the conversation proceeds. An understanding based even partly on guesses or assumptions is dangerous. But ask questions diplomatically – avoid saying, "You didn't explain that properly."
- Remain unemotional: too much thinking ahead (However can I overcome that point?) can distract you.
- Concentrate: allow nothing to distract you.

- Look at the other person: nothing is read more rapidly as lack of interest than an inadequate focus of attention – good eye contact is essential (and furthermore, in negotiating, a lack of it will always be read as deviousness).
- Mentally note key points: edit what you hear so that you can better retain key points manageably.
- Avoid personalities: do not let your view of someone as a person distract you from the message, or from dealing with them if that is necessary.
- Do not lose yourself in subsequent arguments: some thinking ahead may be useful; too much and you may suddenly find you have missed something.
- Avoid negatives: beginning with clear signs of disagreement (even a dismissive look) can make the other person clam up and destroy the dialogue.
- Make written notes: do not trust your memory, and if it is appropriate to do so, ask permission before writing the other party's comments down.

Make no mistake, if you listen – *really* listen – then everything that follows will be a little easier and more certain. If you pick up 100 per cent of the message, you are in a much better position to respond effectively. There is a good reason why we are equipped with two ears and one mouth!

Rookie Buster

There is a good reason why we are equipped with two ears and one mouth!

Asking questions

Always ask sufficient questions to help you with the whole process. Ask about the other person, their situation, their needs and their priorities. Open questions, those which cannot be answered simply by "yes" or "no" and that tend to start with "what", "where", "why", "how" or "who", are usually best. They get people talking and produce more information. This will give you the raw material for your case.

It is difficult to find a black cat in a dark coal cellar, until it scratches you. Similarly, it is difficult to negotiate if there are too many gaps in your knowledge about the situation. You may just find yourself boxed into a corner. If in doubt, ask, and ask at once; if you let the moment pass, it may be impossible to check later without appearing weak.

Rookie Buster

If in doubt, ask, and ask at once; if you let the moment pass, it may be impossible to check later without appearing weak.

Reading body language

We have looked at reading between the lines of what is said, but words, tone and emphasis are not the only means by which messages are conveyed when you speak to someone. People project all sorts of non-verbal clues to their feelings. Some of these are routine: a nod intended to mean "yes", a grunt obviously expressing derision. We normally take these in our stride, though in negotiation they must not be missed. Body language may be an inexact science, but it is interesting and worth some study. One gesture is not an infallible sign of anything. An unbuttoned jacket may only mean it is a tight fit; wearing a jacket at all may be a response to fierce air conditioning rather than an indication of formality.

It is worth keeping an eye on body language through the whole
process of negotiation. You should not over-react to anything, or inter-
pret one gesture as an infallible sign of something, but you must not
ignore indications that could be useful either. Proceed with care. The
list that follows gives an indication of what is involved.

Open-mindedness	Wariness
Shown by:	*Shown by*:
Open hands	Arms crossed on chest
Unbuttoned jacket	Legs over chair arm while seated
	Sitting in reversed armless chair
	Crossed legs
	Fist-like gestures
	Pointing the index finger
	Making karate-like chopping gestures

Thinking/analysing	Confidence
Shown by:	*Shown by*:
Hand to face gestures	Steepling of the hands
Tilted head	Hands on back of head
Stroking chin	(authority position)
Peering over glasses	Back stiffened
Taking glasses off, cleaning them	Hands in jacket pockets, with
Earpiece of glasses in mouth	thumbs outside
Getting up from the table and walking around	Hands on lapels of jacket
Putting hand to bridge of nose	

Territorial dominance
Shown by:
Feet on desk
Feet on chair
Leaning against/touching object
Placing object in a desired space
Hands behind head, leaning back

Nervousness
Shown by:
Clearing throat
"Whew" sound
Whistling
Picking/pinching flesh
Fidgeting in chair
Hands covering mouth while
　speaking
Not looking at the other person
Tugging at clothes while seated
Jingling money in pockets
Tugging at ear
Perspiration/wringing of hands

Frustration
Shown by:
Short breaths
Tutting sound
Tightly clenched hands
Wringing hands
Fist-like gestures
Pointing index finger
Running hand through hair
Rubbing back of neck

Boredom
Shown by:
Doodling
Drumming fingers
Legs crossed, with kicking foot
Head in palms of hands
Blank stare (especially out of the
　window!)

Acceptance
Shown by:
Hand to chest
Open arms and hands
Touching gestures
Moving closer to another
Preening

Expectancy
Shown by:
Rubbing palms together
Jingling money in pockets
Crossed fingers
Moving closer

Suspicion	**Alertness/attention**
Shown by:	*Shown by*:
Not looking at you	Hands on hips
Arms crossed	Hands on mid-thigh when
Moving away from you	seated
Positioning the body (and	Sitting on edge of chair
attention) away from direct	Arms spread, gripping edge of
contact with the other person	table
Sideways glance	
Touching/rubbing nose	
Rubbing eye(s)	
Buttoning jacket	
Drawing away	

Remember that body language can only offer clues and should not become a fixation, though if the signs appear to match with what is being said, the indication is likely to be accurate.

The overriding reason for being sensitive to what is said, and to nuances, gestures and so on, is to help you stay in line with the two basic factors of negotiation:

- Your plan.
- Your reading of how things are going and being received.

Local customs

There are plenty of other things to concentrate on as well.

Consider this example. A European visitor has had some correspondence with the general manager of a local organization in Singapore and a meeting is arranged there. The European is greeted cordially, offered a drink and as the meeting seems about to get under way he is given a business card. He tucks it quickly into his top pocket and begins to state his case.

A small point, but the ritual of business card exchange is important in the East. It is expected that you will study a card, treat it as

116   important and store it safely. Certainly you need to hand over one of
your own in exchange. Not doing so will not make the discussion collapse in ruins, but failure to understand local conditions may have a
negative effect that will add to the balance against you.

The moral: it pays to check such local differences of behaviour and
social nuance. It is one thing to check currency rates and tariffs, it is
another to remember not to point your feet at someone in case it
causes offence, as in Buddhist countries. So if you plan to deal internationally, you must take the trouble to understand the specific local
culture in which you are working.

Rookie Buster

If you plan to deal internationally, you must take the
trouble to understand the specific local culture in which
you are working.

Reacting to the other party's tactics

The following descriptions of various ploys may help you. They show
some of the tactics you may face, and suggest what the other party
hopes for as a result, and your possible response.

Other party's behaviour	Hoping you will	Your action
Chaos (Displays anger, storms out, takes umbrage)	Apologize, give concession, or get angry (and thus more vulnerable) yourself	Keep calm, express your concern at any misunderstanding, seek clarification, and let things return to normal before trying to proceed
Poor me (Plea for special sympathy, concern or approach because of their situation)	Give more away because you feel sorry for them	Do not be put off or be overly sympathetic; acknowledge the problem, restate your position and then take the conversation back on track
Not me (Claims they cannot make decision, must refer to boss, spouse, committee, etc.)	Yield to pressure without souring relations: "it is not my fault"	Ask questions to ascertain whether it is true or just a ploy. In some meetings it may be worth checking early on as to whether they have the authority to make an arrangement

118

Other party's behaviour	Hoping you will	Your action
Only option (Keeps suggesting unacceptable option, without alternative)	Be forced into agreement, seeing no option	Keep calm, bear your objectives firmly in mind, suggest other alternatives such as a middle ground, and keep setting out the problem
No way (Immediately stating one element as non-negotiable)	Give up or offer a great deal to try to make it negotiable	Offer to set that element aside, moving on to other things and getting back to it once rapport is established and agreement is clear on some other elements
What??? (Overreaction to something; shock-horror to indicate impasse)	Offer a rapid concession to compensate	Ignore the first response and restate the issue to prompt a more considered, informative response

Other party's behaviour	Hoping you will	Your action
Can't (Opens with an initial, intractable problem: e.g. you can't do anything unless the project can be completed by the end of the month)	Concede	Ask questions to establish the truth; it is more likely to be an initial stance, so refer to the other variables
No-can-do (Contains no detail or reason, but is very negative: "That's just not at all acceptable")	See it as intractable and give in	Ask for detail, why it is unacceptable, how different it needs to be. Get away from the unspecific and down to the facts
Something more (An overt request for some extra benefit)	Give it to gain goodwill and keep things going	Investigate the trading possibilities. "If I give you X, would you be able to agree to Y?"

Other party's behaviour	Hoping you will	Your action
Policy (The rules are quoted: more than my job's worth – company policy, for example)	Read it as unchangeable and not even try to negotiate	Check whether it is true, whether there are exceptions or others have authority to make them. Rules are made to be broken but be prepared for this to be difficult on occasion and, if necessary, to leave it
Sell me (Negotiation is dependent on a tacit agreement, e.g. to buy or take action. If the deal is put in question, the whole situation may be changing)	Give in to secure agreement	Ask questions; do you need go back to the stage of persuasion? Find out if it is a ploy. If so, stick to your position and push back hard
Big vs. little (A big deal is made of a small point, and then used as a concession for something they really want)	See the first as a real issue and trade, in a way that is not a good exchange	Check real importance, compare and deal with the two things together

Other party's behaviour	Hoping you will	Your action
No progress (Things appear to be deadlocked; no clear way out)	Give in as only way forward	Suggest a real change, a break, an arbitrator. If it is a ploy, these may be resisted and you can get back on track

As your experience of negotiating grows, it may be worth keeping notes of your own examples of such things, as an aide-memoire for the future.

Getting results

There are several aspects to negotiation. The process itself is important, and the structure and sequence of events also contribute to its success. The ritual may be important too, and the techniques certainly are, but it is ultimately people that make it work, so no aspect of interpersonal behaviour must be overlooked.

Any difficulty is likely to be less because the individual elements are themselves complex, than because of the problem of orchestrating the whole thing and missing details. Again, a short case scenario helps make the point.

John makes use of interpersonal behaviour

John is a department head in a busy local government office. Certain matters have to be agreed by his superior, James, before John can proceed on them alone. The two generally work well together, partly through experience and having the measure of each other. John understands, for example, the amount of detail his boss needs to see before

122   letting go. One fault James has is that he hates to say no, even when it is right to do so. He will talk and talk until shortage of time and the fact that they are both busy leads to matters being left. Today he is doing just that, endlessly bypassing a decision about something John wants to get under way fast.

John decides to meet the issue head on. Once it is clear what is happening, he stands up.

He looks James straight in the eye, and says, "Perhaps I should forget it, but you do want to get the appraisal system revised before the year end, don't you?"

James is brought up short, both by the action and the fact that the question relates to something quite different from their discussion.

"Yes, of course," he says; "that's surely agreed."

John interrupts. "Yes, it is, but you are never going to achieve it if this other matter isn't cleared up fast. Now what I suggest is …"

John has taken command and reset the agenda, and now has much more likelihood of getting a decision. This was not purely because of what was said, though this may have helped. It was principally through the impact of something purely behavioural. Just saying it politely would not have had the same impact.

This is just one aspect of the power of interpersonal behaviour in negotiating. Such a scenario makes useful points, so ask yourself:

- How can you use behavioural factors to avoid dangers that are created for you in negotiation?
- Similarly, how can you spot opportunities to increase your power and influence in negotiation using such factors?
- What particular factors do you think you can identify and use that play to your style and strengths?

Coach's notes

Those who get every aspect moving together as a co-ordinated whole are likely to make the best and most effective negotiators. So you must:

- Concentrate throughout any negotiation meeting. There will always be a great deal to take in.
- Keep your ears and eyes open for any sign, any nuance that might assist you in the process.
- Remember that behavioural factors can give warning of dangers, allowing you to take action to avoid them, and highlight opportunities, allowing you to strengthen the effectiveness of what you do.

Go for it! Negotiation demands constant fine-tuning. Just as in a sailing boat a hand needs to be kept on the tiller to compensate for wind and tide and maintain smooth progress towards a destination, so it is with negotiation. However well planned your tactics, you are constantly having to respond to the other party. Sometimes this means dealing with something you expected, at least at some point and in some form, and which you can be prepared for. On other occasions it means responding quickly to unexpected things.

The overall objective is to remain on course. You are heading towards your objectives whatever happens, though there may need to be some give and take. It is important that any response you make is, whilst prompt, also considered. Some of this can only come with practice. It is always worth analysing what went well, what went less well, and what there is to learn from a negotiation, whatever the outcome.

Notes

Although the nature of negotiations can vary widely, and certainly too much to allow us to cover the entire range of possibilities here, many have contractual or legal implications. This chapter sets out how to approach the contractual side of things. Here you can see how to introduce this element of the discussions and handle it in an appropriate manner. But remember – anything to do with legalities needs great care.

CHAPTER 8

Dotting the i's

Finding the right format

Some negotiations, however hard fought, are essentially informal. No elaborate record of proceedings is necessary, and both parties are content to implement whatever has been agreed. The discussion may be only brief, and, once concluded, quickly forgotten.

Other negotiations may need to state clear arrangements, without necessarily having to be in writing. It should, though, be noted that a verbal contract can be binding in a court of law (as can an email). Consider this category very carefully. Check as to whether anything formal is in fact necessary. Formalities are less necessary when all goes well, in which case goodwill may be enough to see things through. They exist to provide for situations that change or have not been foreseen. Such things might include, for example, a change of personnel in a company. It is clearly a problem if the person with whom you make a clear, but informal, arrangement is no longer in the job when a problem occurs; the problem will be worse if the new person is not only ignorant of the arrangement, but hostile to it.

With other negotiations, it may be essential to document the agreement. Often the setting out of terms and conditions, or other arrangements, is intended to be formal and contractual, and is very necessary. Once agreed the parties are stuck with them. No review of negotiating would therefore be complete without some comment on this aspect of the process. When documentation is necessary, it is important to get it right. Be warned: any omissions in contracts can cost you dear; the details matter.

Rookie Buster

Be warned: any omissions in contracts can cost you dear; the details matter.

The purpose of a contract

The purpose of a contract is to protect. It secures against what might happen if – for whatever reason or circumstance – the agreement is not implemented. Sometimes the penalty is considerable; if terms and conditions are not met, a significant amount of money may be lost.

For example, if you book a wedding reception, and then the bride and groom fall out and there is no wedding after all, there may still be a large bill to pay. The venue owners, perhaps unable to re-let the facility at short notice, may invoke the conditions of the agreement and protect themselves against such loss of income.

Making contracts acceptable

For a contractual situation to be acceptable, and not seen as inappropriate, draconian or otherwise unsuitable, certain factors are important. If you are introducing the need for a contract, make sure that what you do:

- Is communicated clearly with no possibility of misunderstandings.

- Enhances the relationship involved, if necessary on a continuing
  basis.
- Allows the progressing and securing of agreement to proceed
  effectively and promptly.
- Still allows any necessary flexibility within the arrangement.
- Links logically and neatly to the practicalities involved.

Setting policy

In an organization of any size, your first question may be to find out
who makes policy decisions and whom you will need to consult. If you
are in charge of such matters yourself, fine; even if you are not, you
may still have an input to make. Look out for any circumstances not
covered by existing policy, and be ready to feed back information that
may prompt policy changes or updates.

An example is the wedding reception referred to above. The venue
may decide that stricter terms and conditions, and higher penalties for
cancellation, are necessary at certain times of the year. A wedding
function lost in, say, February is perhaps more damaging than in peak
season when a substitute may be more easily found.

Addressing the essentials

Contractual arrangements need to make clear:
- The basis of the agreement.
- The terminology to be used by both parties (for instance, is
  postponing a wedding different from cancelling it?).
- All elements of dates, timing and deadlines.
- The procedures, documentation and administration involved.
- All financial matters in unambiguous detail.

Be thorough, think through the details and make sure they are
comprehensively included up front.

Rookie Buster

Be thorough, think through the details and make sure they are comprehensively included up front.

Introducing contractual matters

A contract may cause problems if it also causes surprise. If you produce a ten-page document for signature after hours of debate and discussion that contained no mention of the need for it, people will twitch; rightly so. You must make matters clear from the beginning.

- Do not apologize for the arrangement, though you may need to explain its necessity.
- Stress the mutual advantages.
- Use language that stresses the joint benefits of clarity; for example, talk about working together.
- Plan to mention the contractual side progressively, sufficiently early, and set the scene for any detailed discussion about it that may be necessary later.
- Use a checklist to ensure no detail is missed. Make sure all necessary information is to hand, or secured and recorded if it is to be part of the agreement.

The process is progressive, and dealing with it may well spread throughout the meeting, rather than being confined to one self-contained section.

Dealing with contractual matters

This is often a crucial element of many negotiation discussions. A systematic approach to dealing with contractual matters is best, and it creates the greatest likelihood of ensuring that no problems or objections ensue.

Rookie Buster

A systematic approach to dealing with contractual matters is best.

Step-by-step

The following ten key points will help you incorporate planning for the contract into the whole of the proceedings:

- Introduce the concept of contract. This needs to be carefully timed. The right moment may pass, and it will then get more difficult to say "We must have this in writing." Waiting for the other party to raise this may not be best; you have to plan and be prepared to move the conversation on to the issue. The first time you mention a contract may simply be in order to gain agreement on the need for discussion about it. It may also prompt a decision about how and when in the meeting this will be done.
- Make sure details are clear. This is an area for crystal clear communication. For instance, there can be different interpretations of one word: when does "provisional" become "permanent"? Any such confusion may cause disproportionately greater problems later.
- Make figures and timing especially clear. Both these are worth being really pedantic about. For example, when, exactly, is the end of the month or year? Again, misunderstanding of such a detail can cause real problems.

132

- Check understanding. This may be as simple as just saying "Is that clear?" occasionally, but it is always very important. Do not assume that matters are clearly understood between you. You need to know with certainty that they are.

- Document your side of arrangements. Make things clear, agree them, then say how you will confirm it, and do just that. Delays can cause confusion. It may also help precision of agreement if you take the initiative: write things down in detail, then the other side can simply say they agree. Sometimes you may want to do this the other way around to save you time, as with a supplier, for example: get them to document the details so that you can agree, but always read the small print carefully.

- Ask for their confirmation. Do not assume this will come automatically: ask for it. And chase it up if necessary. If contractual arrangements are understood and agreed, you do not have to be circumspect about this: indeed, any dilatory behaviour at this stage may be a warning sign that you will want to note.

- Chase for action. This is crucial. If people ignore some key stage, do not feel awkward about reminding them. To make sure you do not forget, if matters stretch over some time, put a note in your diary about what is needed when. Remember that delay may well be in the other party's interest.

- Adopt the right manner. Always take a positive approach to contractual matters, stressing that they are important and that they are there to help both parties. Deal with them in a way that appears efficient and professional, and you will achieve what you want in the smoothest possible way.

- Link to the future. An agreement and contract made today set the scene for the future. You may want to begin to touch on future arrangements as you tie down a current one. This can pay dividends in the long run.

Being on the receiving end 133

You will not always be the one introducing contractual matters, of course. When such things are put to you, the rules are also straightforward:

- Listen to, read and check everything that is proposed, to make sure you truly understand.
- Take time, if necessary, to consider or to confer with someone else, including, if appropriate, someone with appropriate legal expertise.
- Be absolutely sure that you can live with the implications, including those of the worst case scenario, before you sign anything.
- Remember that if someone is pushing you to sign and conclude matters with undue haste, this could be a sign that more thought is necessary.

And finally, in contracts more than anywhere; never agree to something in haste; you may well find yourself repenting at leisure.

Rookie Buster

In contracts more than anywhere: never agree to something in haste; you may well find yourself repenting at leisure.

Tackling breakdown

If you deal with contractual matters in the right kind of way there should be minimal problems. But what if something contractual is agreed and then the other party fails to comply in some way? If breakdown occurs, what is to be done should be tackled at once, not least so that you can take a lead in making suggestions. There are three options.

1. **Apply the letter of the law**. The first option is simply to stick to

134 the terms exactly. That is what they are there for. They were agreed. There is no need to feel bad about invoking the conditions. Sometimes this approach will go unchallenged and cause no problems. If not, or if you are worried about souring future arrangements, you may need to take some other action.

2. **Negotiate a compromise**. If you feel so inclined, you can be generous and insist on less than the full terms. You may make some other arrangement that will foster goodwill without losing anything significant. If the situation is reversed, you may want to insist this is done, to minimize damage to your side (and this may necessitate a mini-negotiation within the negotiation).

3. **Make an exception**. This third option is really a variant of the compromise above. In the example of the wedding referred to earlier, a postponement at a time when another booking can be easily obtained may guarantee the rescheduled date and introduce considerable goodwill in a business dependent to a large degree on recommendation. It may be important to make it clear that what is done is an exception and that this sets no precedents for the future. If this point is strongly made, you may be seen as very reasonable, and this may lead to a return compromise in future.

Rookie Buster

If breakdown occurs, what is to be done should be tackled at once, not least so that you can take a lead in making suggestions.

Getting it right

Let's look at an example to show how important it is to deal with this in the right way.

Charles and Jackie think they have agreed

Charles works for a government agency, giving advice to and providing support services in developing countries. He has people under his control going to and fro undertaking projects in a dozen different countries. He is meeting a sales executive from an international hotel group to secure a corporate rate that will save money, yet allow him to accommodate his people suitably.

Jackie is the sales executive. She is keen to do a deal, and knows there is a worthwhile amount of business to be had if she does.

Their meeting looks at the volume of business, the locations involved, the rates and discounts involved, the facilities provided. For example, Charles needs to be sure his people can always operate computers and access the internet in their rooms.

Using the ploy of concentrating on the rates, and the savings he must make, Charles gets Jackie to the point of doing a deal, then throws in a last-minute request: "Of course, this will only be acceptable if executive grade rooms are guaranteed." He knows that these rooms include free broadband access. Jackie vaguely agrees. She sees the profitability of the deal declining and kicks herself for letting the ploy work, and her last word on the matter is non-committal: "I'll see what I can do." When they part, each is content that the deal agreed works for them.

Later, when the new arrangement is supposed to be under way, Charles sees in an email from one of his people in Africa that on arrival at their hotel they found that only a basic grade of room had been reserved for them. As a result, the email had to be sent through the hotel business centre and was delayed by some hours.

Why the problem?

The answer is simple; there was nothing in writing. Or, at least nothing that set out the full details point by point. Charles thought he had prompted an extra concession by using a clever ploy. Jackie, who had not actually promised anything, thought it had been forgotten and done no more about it.

Even in so simple a situation, such a failing (and both parties here were at fault) can cause problems. In this case it may only necessitate a small change to the arrangement. But even if Jackie now includes the upgrade, will Charles ever be quite so happy about the deal? It will no doubt change the situation when the contract needs renewing a year hence.

It is easy to imagine the possible confusion when much more detailed contractual arrangements are part of negotiation. So always be circumspect in this area and ask:

- What points need deciding and including in any policy for contractual matters you may have?
- Do you have clear information available as a prompt to discussion – a checklist, for example, to ensure you do not miss any tricks?
- How much documentation does your situation demand, and does it need origination or review?

Always ensure you have something in writing *whenever* it may be necessary, and that what you have will do the job.

Rookie Buster

Always ensure you have something in writing *whenever* it may be necessary, and that what you have will do the job.

Coach's notes

The trick here is to balance the need to avoid immediate losses with the need for advantages of a more long-term nature. You need to:

- Decide appropriate policy and introduce contractual matters into any meeting in a way that sets the scene for what you want to do.
- Be sensitive to the details involved and ensure mutual understanding of the full picture.
- Adopt a systematic approach to the way contractual matters are integrated into the discussion.
- Check and check again before you sign anything.
- Balance advantages against disadvantages when applying the letter of the law, if it becomes necessary to do so.

138

Go for it! When I set up Touchstone Training & Consultancy, for part of its existence the business was a partnership. My fellow partner and I had known each other and worked together for twenty years. Working out how things would be handled between us needed a little care, but was readily agreed and pretty straightforward. At an early meeting with our accountant we were asked about our "partnership agreement"; we explained it was all agreed, but not very formal. The accountant became very stern, recommending we put something in writing: "In case one of you goes ga-ga," he said. We did. Although we both avoided madness during the partnership, it was good advice, because it recognized that in a small business, if one partner was incapacitated in any way it would be left to others (friends, family, colleagues or professional advisers) to sort matters out. You need a very good reason *not* to have something in writing; just as much as the reverse, in fact.

Notes

Enough has been said by now to demonstrate that negotiation is a practical art. It is one thing to dissect and discuss it, but quite another to put it into practice. In this chapter we'll consider a case that is illustrated in an actual conversation, linked to a commentary about what is going on. This shows how a meeting should be planned and how techniques can be appropriately deployed to make it work. (The conversation is based on a role-play exercise undertaken by two of my training colleagues to create a demonstration during a negotiating training course.)

CHAPTER 9

Linking theory and practice

Every negotiation you are involved with can potentially teach you something useful for the future – all you have to do is think about what happened and make sure you use the lessons.

Case study

The background

First, some information to set the scene.

Pat, a freelance journalist, writes articles and company material and does some public relations work. Working partly from home, her business is thriving; so much so that she has decided that she needs to replace the now aging equipment she has at home by a more up-to-date computer and printer. After some research she has decided on the equipment that will suit her. She has received a quotation from an office equipment firm, and has asked their salesman to visit her to discuss it. With experience of writing about business topics, and having met many business managers during her work, some

142 professional techniques have rubbed off on her and she is determined to get a good deal.

Jean helps Pat on a part-time basis. Jean will also use any new equipment, and must be able to do so productively and successfully. Being older than Pat, she is a little wary of anything that is different from what she is used to. Pat wants to keep Jean happy, and plans to make sure that the change is something that she will ultimately be happy with.

John is confident of a deal. John works for Computer Clobber. He is an experienced salesman. He understands the equipment he sells, he is keen to make a sale, and he knows he must strike a satisfactory deal if he is to get the business. From his previous conversation with Pat, he believes that she likes the package of equipment he has recommended; he confidently expects to conclude the deal at the scheduled meeting. He looks forward to receiving his commission.

Pat sees two tasks ahead.

First, she needs to sit down with Jean and discuss the matter. She has three reasons for this:

- To make sure that Jean feels involved. If Jean thinks the new equipment is something she helped select, then she is more likely to accept the change.
- Pat wants to check if Jean can think of anything that may affect the need they have for the equipment and what it can do.
- She wants to try out some thoughts about her meeting with the salesman.

Two heads are better than one. Pat is sensible enough to realize she must sit down quietly and prepare for the meeting. John does this for a living; she feels she could easily be taken advantage of, but is determined to get a good deal. Thereafter, knowing that Jean feels better about the planned change, and with some notes to work from at the meeting, Pat is ready for the next stage.

Details 143

The case study describes a simplified commercial situation. Such a process would be essentially similar in a non-commercial environment or where any two people must negotiate. In this conversation, the decision to purchase has already been made, provided Pat can get the sort of deal she wants. If she cannot, she would be prepared to talk to another supplier instead. Below is what each protagonist plans to get from the meeting.

- Pat wants to keep costs down. Pat has debated long and hard with herself about what she can afford. It is very important to her to have something good. She wants the larger and faster of the two printers she has checked out. Above all she would like to minimize the cost. Yet by going into the matter she has also realized there are additional items, such as extra software, that could be worth obtaining as well. The specifications in the quote include two additional software packages as well as what is bundled with the deal. Also Pat is worried about being away from her desk for any training that may be necessary.

- John is confident of a sale. John believes he is close to an order. The equipment seems to be exactly what is wanted and he has offered a reasonable deal. He has some leeway on price, either in terms of a reduction or juggling with other elements of the package, but wants a profitable sale. He sees it as the last part of the sales process rather than a negotiation. He is mistaken in this view and is therefore not as prepared as he should be.

Looking out for variables

A number of elements are used as variables during the conversation. These include: the equipment itself; the software; delivery and installation; training; payment terms; price and discount; and even publicity. The principle of analysing what you do after a meeting and seeing what lessons there may be for the future – things to build on and things to avoid – helps accelerate your experience.

Rookie Buster

The principle of analysing what you do after a meeting and seeing what lessons there may be for the future helps accelerate your experience.

The ebb and flow of negotiation

(Note: Comments in italics appear periodically about the conversation as it proceeds. There are also occasional numbers in brackets marking various stages; these link to a checklist later in the chapter.)

Let's make them comfortable (though maybe in reality a sales person would not expect this). Imagine that John is sitting in Pat's office. The initial greetings and polite inquiries are over, Pat has brought them coffee, and John now takes the initiative and turns to business.

JOHN: You got your quote, then?

PAT: Yes, thanks very much.

JOHN: I hope you found it interesting. *(John tests to discover her initial attitude.)*

PAT: Yes, indeed. I am not sure it is exactly right and I am comparing it with some others, but it was certainly clear. (1) *(She indicates that she is looking at other quotes, and hints that they are also good, perhaps better.)*

JOHN: I see. In what way is ours not quite right? *(He attempts to clarify her last remark.)*

PAT: Technically I am sure it is quite good. I am not a technical person (2), of course, but you seem to have reflected my brief well enough and I have no quibbles with that. However, I am after a total system. Not just the computer itself, but the software, printer and things like training as well. I think it's these areas you need to have a closer look at. *(She begins to soften up John.)*

JOHN: I see. Can you tell me where you see any particular problem? *(He seeks further clarification.)*

PAT: I think there are several areas. Perhaps we can take them one at a time. *(Pat prefers to deal with one thing at a time and in the sequence of her choice. She starts with the other equipment.)* Let's deal with the ancillary equipment first. In your quote you recommend the faster of the two laser printers you discussed. As you know, I really want the faster printer rather than the more basic one if I can, and also a separate hard disc unit to give me secure backup for my files – well, for everything. I would also like to have desktop publishing software on the computer, not least so that I can liaise with a colleague who creates material on that system and extend my work portfolio.

Now what you have suggested will certainly do everything I want – a Rolls Royce job in fact – but that printer does make the whole package more than I really hoped to spend. (3) *(She indicates that the total price is too high.)* I am not sure that the extra software is essential anyway. I could manage without it for a while longer. So what I suggest is that you let me have the desktop publishing software on loan long enough to get familiar with it, test it out and see how it goes. *(Pat asks for a concession, trading something she now describes as of low importance to her: the extra software.)*

JOHN: It is just the additional software that you want on that basis? *(John asks a clarifying question.)*

PAT: Yes. If I do want to keep it, then it will postpone the payment for that element for just a while, and that means I can go for the better printer. See what I mean? *(This was always her intention.)*

JOHN: Yes, I do.

PAT: It won't be difficult for you to arrange that (4), I'm sure, and if I decide in favour you will get payment for it anyway in, say, six months. *(Pat minimizes the difficulty the point may make for him.)*

JOHN: Okay, I suppose I can arrange that. I'm pretty sure you will want to keep it anyway. *(He concedes what appears to be a small point.)*

PAT: *(Pat confirms the concession and turns to her second point – more about software...)* I expect you're right. Good, that's fine. Let's turn now to the question of the other software I would like. I would ideally like the graphics package, and the one that will do my accounts as well as word processing and the usual bundle of stuff. Would you be able to include those at no extra charge? *(... and asks for a concession.)* They are not very costly but I must keep the overall cost down, as I've said.

JOHN: You didn't include those in the spec you gave me – or did you? *(John begins to resist)*

PAT: No, I'm sorry. *(She apologizes, but repeats the request.)* I hadn't been through all the literature at the time, but I can see they would be useful. It would make your overall arrangements much more attractive. (5)

JOHN: It is an extra cost for us, though. *(John continues to resist.)*

PAT: Not very much in terms of the overall cost. *(Pat persists, minimizing the effect involved.)*

JOHN: Well, perhaps not. I guess I could let you have those if you go ahead. *(He agrees, albeit reluctantly, to include the extra software.)*

PAT: And you will deliver that along with everything else and include a run-down on them in the training I need for the additional software? *(She adds a request for a further small related concession.)*

JOHN: Well, I don't know: it will extend the training time and ... *(John realizes he has given away more than he thought.)*

PAT: But they are not much good unless I can work them. I am sure I will pick it up fast and it won't extend the time to any real extent. *(Pat presses the point and minimizes the difficulty – of time and cost.)*

JOHN: All right. *(He agrees.)*

PAT: I appreciate that. Now, what next? Ah yes, the delivery and installation. *(Pat offers a small note of thanks and raises her third point: delivery and installation.)*

JOHN: Well, that should be straightforward. Is that the last point? *(John attempts to get the rest of her shopping list.)*

PAT: Yes. (6) Well, apart from training, but I am sure that's no problem. It's all included and you agreed to run me through the other software. *(Pat belittles what is described as the last point.)*

JOHN: Yes, okay. What about delivery? To here, I suppose? *(Reassured, John goes back to the third point.)*

PAT: That's right. I've ordered one of those desk units to house everything. Once I know which quote I'm going to accept, I can get that and away you go. Your people do install, don't they? I don't want a pile of boxes dumped on the doorstep.

JOHN: Yes, of course. Delivery and installation are all included.

PAT: And you will take away all the boxes and packing? (*Pat asks for a small extra.*)

JOHN: We don't usually do that. Can't you leave them for the dustman? (*Again John resists.*)

PAT: The residents association is a bit strict about that sort of thing and the chairman lives next door. As a matter of fact, he's interested in seeing what equipment I get. If you can get all the boxes taken away, I can possibly recommend you. (7) I believe he is thinking of replacing and extending equipment for his firm. (*Pat hints at future business prospects as a lever to obtain the concession.*)

JOHN: I'm still not sure that I can arrange that. Our despatch manager is very strict.

PAT: See what you can do, will you? (*The point is left hanging, but Pat has a nice case now for saying to whoever delivers, "John said he'd fix it."*)

JOHN: Okay, I will. Now, what about training? If you decide to go ahead today, then I can get a date in the diary for you to visit the training centre. (*John tries to move to the last point and explains what needs to be done.*)

PAT: And you think a day will be enough, even with the other software included? (*Pat checks details.*)

JOHN: Oh yes, certainly. How about the week after next? (*John goes for agreement.*)

PAT: Hang on, I was hoping you could get your trainer to come here. Would that be possible? (*Pat introduces another request for another concession.*)

JOHN: It is certainly possible, but there would be an extra cost. (*This time John is determined to give nothing away.*)

PAT: You remember I mentioned earlier the other quotes I have? (8)

JOHN: Yes.

PAT: One of the differences is that they are both willing to do the training here. It means I don't have to leave my phone unattended. That's

148   important to someone working on their own. If you schedule the
date well ahead, it would minimize the inconvenience. (*Pat makes
him feel uncompetitive just at the stage when he believes that everything is agreed, and also minimizes the problem.*)

JOHN: Even so, we have a clear scale of charges for in-house visits, and
with what I have already agreed … (*John resists.*)

PAT: I see the problem, but it would be a pity to fall out at this stage.
Everything else seems fine. May I make a suggestion? (*Pat stresses
how close John is to a firm order.*)

JOHN: What, exactly? (*John tries to clarify.*)

PAT: I have been asked by one of the office equipment journals [she
names a well known one] to write a feature on how writers use
computers. If I buy yours, I shall have to use it as an example – after
all, it will be the only one I've got! (*Pat makes the request seem to
have clear compensations – she sells it.*) If I promise to mention your
company by name, do you think your boss would agree to the training being done here? It would be such a help. At least ask him; he
might like the idea. Right? (9)

JOHN: I can certainly ask. It sounds a good swap to me. Will you leave
it with me? (*John agrees – conditionally.*)

PAT: Yes, of course. See what reaction you get.

JOHN: Right. So you seem to be agreed. We let you have the additional
software on six months' loan, and I will work on the training being
done here.

PAT: And on getting all the boxes cleared away – yes?

JOHN: That's right, I nearly forgot. Can you go ahead on that basis?
(*John aims to wrap up the deal.*)

PAT: Yes, I think we can … but there is just one small thing. Again, this
is included in the other quotes. That's insurance. (*Pat raises a new
issue – a "small thing".*)

JOHN: What do you mean? (*John queries it.*)

PAT: They offer a year's free insurance as part of the package.

JOHN: On the same machine and costing?

PAT: Not exactly, I suppose, but similar. (*Pat concedes that it is not like
for like.*)

JOHN: You have to look at the overall deal, you know. With the price

we have quoted and the extras there is no possibility of my matching that. (*John gives a firm refusal.*)

PAT: Well, I suppose I have to accept that. Even so it is a bit of a disap-
pointment. Your company offers the best arrangements in many
ways, but even with the items you have agreed it is still not the most
competitive. I take it you do want the business? (*Pat suggests that
she is in fact being very reasonable – and raises a price objection.*)

JOHN: Yes, indeed we do.

PAT: Perhaps you would consider adjusting the overall discount to
make up for my having to fix and pay for insur-
ance separately? (*Pat changes to a new suggestion to save her money.*)

JOHN: I believe our original price was very
keen. We do, as I said, want the order, but I
don't really have any more leeway over the discount. (*John resists.*)

PAT: I'm sure your price is keen, but as I said it is not the
most competitive. (*Pat again reminds him he is in
competition with other suppliers – she pauses to
prompt a response.*)

JOHN: What sort of difference are you talking about?

PAT: To really make everything you have said add up to the best deal
all round, I suppose the discount would need to go up by seven and
a half per cent or so. (*Pat puts some numbers in the ring.*)

JOHN: That's a lot of money, and the margins on this kind of system are
not so great. (*John resists again.*)

PAT: How far could you go? (*But Pat squeezes him.*)

JOHN: Myself? I think with what we have already agreed I could not go
beyond four per cent at this stage. That would be my limit.

PAT: And how far could your company go at the next stage? (10) (*Pat
takes him literally, assuming that there may be more to go for and
checks for the limit.*)

JOHN: "At this stage" was just a turn of phrase. Four per cent would be
the company's limit. (*John is wise to that.*)

PAT: No good me calling your boss, you mean? (*It seems an offhand
remark, but Pat is checking his status and authority.*)

JOHN: No, I'm afraid not.

PAT: But you can go to four per cent more discount?

JOHN: Yes, I can.

PAT: I hoped you would go to seven and a half per cent to match the others completely, but let's see what you have agreed. You will include the external hard drive and invoice after six months for the desktop publishing package at the current price, you will include the other software, find out about the training and the boxes, and reduce the price by another four per cent. (*Here Pat belittles his offer, but checks through the points to be sure her suggestions are agreed.*)

JOHN: Yes, that's it.

PAT: On that basis, I think we do have a deal. Would you like another coffee while you sort out the paperwork? (*Still in the driving seat, Pat closes the conversation, ensuring that the paperwork is completed before John has any change of mind.*)

With this conversation in mind, we can review the outcome.

Reading the dynamics of the meeting

Pat had thought about what she wanted. She had considered the process that was to be involved. She did not expect the meeting to go exactly as planned, but used the changing circumstances to feel her way through it. She had firm objectives, but had to deal with a dynamic situation as the other party, of course, had their own intentions.

There are still loose ends but the deal has improved markedly. It may be that Pat is depicted as doing better than would be likely (to make a point!); though no doubt the salesman has still got a profitable deal. She handled it well and deserved to win the majority of points. She certainly did better than others, approaching the same process less well prepared, might have done. And she probably did better than John expected – he perhaps left the meeting muttering about customers getting more demanding by the day.

Adding up the score

The outcome might be summarized as follows. John gets his order, of course, but Pat wins a number of concessions:

- Six months' loan of the desktop publishing package, and later payment for it at the current price.
- Two additional, free, pieces of software.
- The boxes and packing taken away on delivery (perhaps).
- Training at her home, rather than at the training centre, probably, including more training than was originally indicated. (She could have opted to make her order conditional on this).
- An additional four per cent discount.

She has not managed to get free insurance, and has offered collaboration on an article, and tacitly promised a recommendation to a friend. In fact, Pat has saved enough to finance the printer she really wanted and still come out ahead. She led the process and worked through systematically. She was prepared. She negotiated. John, on the other hand, emerges sadder but wiser. He has the order, it may even be reasonably profitable, but he is no doubt saying to himself, "If only …"

Reading the signs

All negotiation will have a subtext of hidden meaning. Some words disguise the true feeling, some can draw attention to the fact that all is not quite as it seems.

The numbers in the conversation indicate some examples of this. Here are the possible real meanings of each of the numbered phrases.

(1) … it was certainly clear.   *(But not exactly right)*

(2) I am not a technical person …   *(You can handle me easily)*

(3) … does make the whole package more than I really hoped to spend …   *(I may not buy unless I get a better deal)*

152

(4) It won't be difficult for you …	(*A little flattery*)
(5) … make your overall arrangement much more attractive.	(*Without it, it is less or not at all attractive*)
(6) Yes.	(*For the moment*)
(7) … I can possibly …	(*Nothing promised. No degree of likelihood*)
(8) Remember … the other quotes.	(*I'm not decided yet; don't lose the order at this stage*)
(9) He might like the idea.	(*And thank you for it*)
(10) … at the next stage.	(*Can anyone else in your organization decide differently?*)

Fine-tuning your approach

The first direction springs from the thinking done and the plan made prior to the meeting. As the conversation above shows, negotiating is a dynamic affair. You can never be sure of what will happen. Even quite minor variances from what is expected or planned can necessitate changes to how the meeting is then handled.

Such changes produce opportunities and challenges. The good negotiator is quick on their feet and always remains open to fine-tuning the approach as the meeting proceeds.

Rookie Buster

The good negotiator is quick on their feet and always remains open to fine-tuning the approach as the meeting proceeds.

And it is always best to assume some fine-tuning will be necessary; no plan can be followed slavishly, as that would ignore the realities of

an essentially interactive process. You will not anticipate everything,   153
nor will you spot every opportunity – but your opponent will not
either. If you can fine-tune in a way that stays a jump ahead, that may
be sufficient to get the deal you want.

Coach's notes

There are certainly some key lessons highlighted here:

- Always have a plan and a clear idea of how you intend to deal with the discussion.
- Resolve to lead whenever possible, though you may not want this to be apparent.
- Fine-tune as you go to bypass difficulties and take advantage of any opportunity that appears unexpectedly along the way.

Go for it! The practical moral of this situation is that to be a successful negotiator you must resolve to:

- Organize your thinking in a way that ensures you keep on track and are able to work to your plan.
- Work in a way that ensures your plan does not act as a straitjacket, but allows for flexibility.
- Anticipate any traps likely to be strewn in your path during the discussion and have appropriate responses ready.
- Manage the inevitable complexity by being familiar with everything that contributes to creating it.

If you know how the process works and approach it in a considered way, this is not only possible, but it will quickly allow you to leave your rookie status far behind – just like Pat.

Notes

....
....
....
....
....
....
....
....
....
....
....
....
....
....
....
....
....
....
....
....
....
....
....
....
....
....
....
....
....
....
....
....

Notes

Negotiation is part art, part science: going about it in the right way increases the likelihood of success. But it does not guarantee success. It is a dynamic, interactive process. It needs to be conducted in a way that is well planned, yet flexible, and recognizing that the people involved are the most important and the least predictable element. The danger with dissecting any such process is that it can then be difficult to put the pieces back together. Now we conclude by pulling together the essentials.

CHAPTER 10

Focusing on the key issues

Orchestrating the overall process

To negotiate successfully you must see the process in the round, take a broad view and continue to do so throughout.

Rookie Buster

To negotiate successfully you must see the process in the round, take a broad view and continue to do so throughout.

This means you must have a good grasp of the principles involved, allowing you to orchestrate and fine-tune as you proceed. Small adjustments along the way can make all the difference to both to the process and to the conclusion.

Summarizing the negotiation process

Here are two checklists, each of them packed to the brim with Rookie Buster tips: the first summarizes overall principles you need, the second your key tactics.

Principles

- Definition: negotiation is about bargaining to reach a mutually agreeable outcome. This is the win–win concept.
- Never neglect your preparation. Have a clear plan but remain flexible.
- Participants must regard each other as equals. Mutual respect is essential to both conduct and outcome.
- There is a need to abide by the rules. Negotiation is about discussion, rather than debate. There is little place for overt one-upmanship or domination, yet each participant must fight their corner.
- Put your cards on the table, at least on major issues. Do not pretend powers or state intentions that are untrue.
- Patience is a key characteristic of the good negotiator. Take your time; do not rush discussion or decision making. Delay is better than a poor outcome.
- Empathy is vital. Put yourself in the other's shoes, see things objectively from their point of view and make sure that your doing so shows.
- State clear objectives. Being open early on about overall intentions can save groping in the dark.
- Avoid confrontation. Do not get into a corner you cannot get out of. Avoid rows and showdowns, but stand firm and keep calm.
- Treat disagreement carefully. Act as devil's advocate, apparently looking at the case from the other person's viewpoint, to avoid a confrontational "I disagree" style.
- Deal with concessions progressively. Where concessions have to

be made, make them unwillingly and one at a time, and trade them.

- Do not let perfection be the enemy of the good. An outcome that is one hundred per cent what you want is rarely an option. Be realistic: do not waste time and effort seeking something out of reach.
- Use openness, but not comprehensively. Declaring your plans and intentions may be useful to the discussion. You may want to keep the motivation behind them hidden.
- Stick with your objectives. Set your sights high and then work at settling as high as possible.
- Know when to drop the whole thing rather than agree a totally inappropriate deal.
- Keep up your guard, maintain your stamina, bide your time. The other party may persevere for hours to see when you will crack.
- Remain professional. For example, respect confidences that are given in the course of negotiations. Such consideration builds relationships and may help you next time.
- Never underestimate people. A velvet glove may be disguising an iron fist.
- End positively. Neither party will get exactly what they want, but if the deal is agreeable, emphasize this at the end.

Keeping the core principles in mind will help you control events and allow you to get nearer to your plan of how – ideally – you want things to go.

Rookie Buster

Keeping the core principles in mind will help you control events and allow you to get nearer to your plan of how – ideally – you want things to go.

162 Key tactics

Like any interactive skill, negotiating is dependent on many factors. These ten are likely to be among the most useful to you. You might like to compose your own list. See how it varies from this, and make sure it reflects exactly the kind of negotiating you do and the kind of people it pits you against.

1. Select the right starting point. Your plan should make it easy for you to take the initiative and quickly get on to your agenda.
2. Aim high, then the trading moves you less far from what you regard as a good position.
3. Do not make your feelings obvious. There is an element of bluff. If your face and body language say that something is minor as you respond to something major, you will do better.
4. Use silence. Some things demand no reaction at all.
5. Watch for early difficulty. Let a rapport and momentum build up before you tackle contentious issues.
6. Do not exaggerate facts. They can be verified, and exaggeration causes problems later.
7. Communicate clearly. Remember the need for understanding as a foundation to the whole process.
8. Be seen to go with the other person's way of doing things, at least to some degree and particularly if you are on their ground.
9. Do not push too hard. There is usually a line beyond which the outcome is not a better deal, but complete breakdown.
10. When negotiation is finished, stop. Once agreement is reached, is clear, agreed and perhaps noted, move on to other matters. Otherwise there is a danger that people may say, "I have been thinking …," and you can be back to square one.

Arriving at the mix of tactics that suits what you are trying to do 163
and helps you towards your goal must be a considered process; it is one
that starts with your planning and also necessitates you being quick on
your feet.

The importance of different factors like these depends on the nature
of the negotiation. Something full of complex financial details poses
different problems from something simpler. You must always match
your chosen method and approach to the nature of a particular
transaction.

Enhancing your approach

A few things to avoid – you will only excel if you *never*:

- Over-react if responses are negative; remember that the other
  person is at pains not to say how excellent every point is.
- Allow yourself to become over-emotional, unpleasant, provocative
  or insulting; a planned and controlled display of emotion may be
  useful (on occasion), but you must know what you are doing.
- Agree to something you do not want; in many situations there is a
  minimal deal which your plan should identify, below which it is
  better to walk away.

Learning from each situation

Every negotiation you conduct can build your expertise, helping you
to fine-tune what works well, what to avoid, what best fits with your
style and what can help in future.

Rookie Buster

Every negotiation you conduct can build your expertise.

164   The detail is important. Sometimes what makes the difference between success and failure is small and seemingly insignificant. One phrase, even one gesture may make such a difference. If all the details are right, the whole will be more likely to work well.

Producing real clout

Negotiation is a topic about which no guide can be comprehensive. It is a dynamic, interactive process, and even the best performance can be made more effective. The key things are to make a start, and to ensure that the experience you gain makes what you do in future better and better.

If you're a driver, the experience of learning to drive is a good example here. Remember your first driving lessons? For a while you probably despaired of ever being able to concentrate on a disparate, long, seemingly endless list of things that all needed doing at once, and make them all work. Negotiation is no different. A basic shopping list of techniques will start you off and allow you to practise. Don't try to do everything at once: try a basic suite of techniques and once you are able to keep control of it, but only then, add to it. Then with the basic techniques in mind you can add to your method of approach and continue to develop it.

Rookie Buster

Don't try to do everything at once: try a basic suite of techniques and once you are able to keep control of it, but only then, add to it.

A good coach, teaching, say, tennis or golf, will always operate this way; whatever your faults and however many you may have, the coach will get you to work on them in a manageable way, probably one at a time. The principle is sound.

Such conscious use of experience in the light of your awareness and $\qquad$ 165
knowledge of the process is the only way to develop real clout. You cannot expect that to come overnight, or without thought or practice.

Here is a final example to help pull the principles in this book together.

Michael seeks promotion

Michael is preparing to go into a meeting with his boss, with the possibility of being promoted. He works in middle management for a financial institution, successfully running a small department. He believes he deserves promotion on the basis both of his success to date, and of his ability to tackle a more demanding job.

Michael knows that the industry he is in has been through dramatic change, including reduced staff levels, in recent years. He knows the demands that higher responsibility will make on him and wants to be sure that he is suitably rewarded for it. He also knows that the organization is currently successful and profitable. In a technical business it makes sense to grow your own management, but he wonders just what this means. Will they be prepared to negotiate, or quickly decide it is better to recruit from outside or select someone else to promote if he pushes for too much?

Gill wants the right person

Gill is the personnel director. She wants to make the right decisions, in order to ensure that the post is filled in a way that will meet the objectives of the job and without disturbing personnel policy or costing too much.

166 Both parties plan their approach

Michael knows enough to plan for the meeting. He considers himself and his strengths relative to the new job, the task itself and the package he considers appropriate. Such a package has plenty of variables: salary, car, expenses, bonuses, medical insurance, pension arrangements, and so on. He also considers things like his new location, staff support, freedom of action, reporting hierarchy and other matters which affect him and his perception of his ability to do a good job.

Next Michael considers his approach and what it will say about him. Too strong and he will be thought difficult; too soft and the personnel director will wonder why these things do not matter to him. He prioritizes the variables: what is a must, a loss leader and so on. He makes some notes, sets an agenda and goes into the meeting ready and confident. He believes he has thought through all the likely scenarios, not least from the point of view of what the other person will do.

Gill also prepares. She wants to be able to confirm the appointment. She too thinks through all that is involved, where to put the emphasis, and is ready and confident. Both parties want something good for the company, yet they are still in a sense adversaries – at least for a while. They are probably equally matched, which reinforces the need for attention to detail in order to secure an edge. A win–win outcome is desirable for both. Michael wants to be able to accept the job and get on with it without regrets about the package. Gill wants him to accept and to move into the new appointment able to give it his full attention. Their aims are not so different.

The way they conduct themselves at the meeting will affect the outcome. Whatever the conclusion, it will not be something that just happened. It will depend on the skills of both and how they each deploy the techniques involved in communication generally, and negotiation in particular. They will make the outcome what it is.

Moving into the real world

As with the case above, so too for you and your negotiations. How well your next negotiating session turns out will depend as much as anything on you. This book has set out to act as a spur to your abilities, but it is what you do now that matters. What you are able to do depends very much on how consciously you set about it. You need to understand and deploy the techniques appropriately. You also need confidence in your ability to do so effectively. We are, I hope, agreed that you can be a better negotiator if you work at it. Indeed, the process of trying will itself help you learn quicker and do better. Continue this process for a while and you will be a match for anyone.

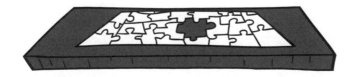

Rookie Buster

What you are able to do depends very much on how consciously you act about it.

Coach's notes

Finally, a few things are worth emphasizing about the ongoing process of developing skills.

- Preparation is key. Preparation really does make a significant difference. Yet it is so easy to miss out, or skimp. Make time for it, think about it, and everything else that follows will be easier.

- Being aware of the process. Try to develop a consciousness of the process. If your mind is actively aware of the overall issues, the complexities and the structure of what is involved, rather than simply moving from point to point, the whole process will be easier. This may seem difficult to begin with. A chess player will concentrate on the current move in the context of the next, the one after, and the opponent's response, all within an overall strategy; such a view is important in negotiation too. It does work and becomes easier to do with practice. In time both the learning process and the deployment of the many techniques will become a habit.

- Becoming confident. Thirdly, remember that confidence is paramount. Planning is the starting point for this. If you have thought about both the principles and the detail of a particular encounter, you will have more confidence in what you plan to do. This will not only help you, but it will be apparent to your opponent and you will come across in a way that will make the whole process easier for you. Confidence is powerful: it sends out signals convincing others that you are a force to be reckoned with, and that can influence the outcome.

Go for it! Some final words of advice:

- Work from a real understanding of the key principles involved in the negotiation process.
- Always see the process as dynamic. Work throughout any meeting to fine-tune how you proceed.
- Stand back and retain the broad view of what is going on, so that you can spot and avoid any pitfalls.
- Consciously use your experience to enhance your approach and maximize what you achieve.

One more thought: never rely on good luck. Good luck is what makes *other people's* negotiations succeed. Yours succeed because of two things – you, and how well you plan and execute the negotiations you conduct.

The tools of the trade

As should by now be clear, the core of negotiating is in trading variables. You must:

- Know what they are (all of them).
- Form a view of their value (to you and your opposite number).
- Keep them in mind and work with them throughout the process.

But there may be a number of variables. It is therefore useful to identify and analyse them, either generally, in terms of what you normally deal with; or for a particular transaction; or both.

As an example of this process and to show some more detail, let's return to the example of the conference manager selling function space. What variables are involved here? And how can we go about listing them?

The first job is to identify the main areas involved in which variables exist. In this example, there might be four categories:

- Finance.
- Logistics.
- Facilities.
- Catering.

Let's look at these in turn and see what there is to trade. First **financial** factors, which might include: credit (long or short); what's included and what isn't (e.g. does room hire include basic visual aid equipment?); invoicing (together or split); deposit; discount (overall or particular, such as a link to a second function); link to timing (does a weekend cost more or less than the week?).

Secondly, **logistical** factors, which might include: timings (e.g. set up the day before? And does event run on into the evening?); cancellation/postponement terms; bedroom accommodation linked to event; ability to rehearse; trial visual aids; parking or collection of participants from the rail station or airport.

Thirdly, **facilities:** these might include: meeting rooms (and syndicate rooms for, say, training events); equipment (from visual aids to microphones); use of other facilities separate from meeting ones (e.g. a hotel might have a swimming pool); computer and internet access facilities.

For **catering**, everything from meals to biscuits and tea/coffee breaks must be considered, also drinks (cash bar?) and aspects of service.

In addition, a host of small details may be significant. Even something like clear (and extra) signage might be a factor and, certainly other things like confidentiality and exclusive use of a venue or some part of it could be involved.

You need to make a similar list that fits your own situation. You may be surprised at how many variables there are. The next stage is to put relative value on them. This may be dependent on knowledge, and thus could change as you find out more. For example, a company planning a new product briefing for their distributors might well regard confidentiality as very important – and be prepared to value it highly if it can be guaranteed.

A systematic and thorough approach, and time set aside to work this through, can put you in a strong position, and there are certainly dangers to an approach that assumes you have it all "in your head" and are simply aiming to wing it. Ultimately success depends on orchestrating such a picture, and you cannot do this unless you see the picture clearly to start with. Many of the techniques reviewed here can be acquired with practice, with a broader range of them being added over time as your confidence builds. But you can always ensure you know your own situation and how you can use the variables involved in what you have to do; and doing so pays dividends in a complex process.

A final thought

If you are the sort of person who always looks at the back of a book first, let me repeat here something from the introduction: I want you to buy this book. You want to be a more effective negotiator. This book will help you become just that – buy it, and we both get what we want. Is it a deal?

Index